NEW CENTURY'S
Encyclopaedia of Economics and Commerce

New Century's

Encyclopaedia of

Economics and Commerce

Volume I

(A to K)

NEW NC CENTURY

New Century Publications

Delhi India

NEW CENTURY PUBLICATIONS
34, Gujranwala Town, Part-2,
Delhi-110 009 INDIA

Tel.: 7138192, 7247805 Tele/Fax: +91-11-7464774
E-mail: indiatax@del2.vsnl.net.in

First Published 2003

ISBN: 81-7708-038-5 (Set)
ISBN: 81-7708-039-3 (Vol. I) ISBN: 81-7708-040-7 (Vol. II)

Published by New Century Publications and printed at Singhal Print Media, Delhi-110 007

PRINTED IN INDIA

Secretarial Assistance
Arun Thesis Typing Centre, Delhi – 110 007

Graphics
Singhal Print Media Pvt. Ltd., New Delhi – 110 005

Contents

A Note on the Encyclopaedia

Economics and Commerce are the two dominant subjects of modern learning. These are, by no means, easy subjects to master. However, an increasing number of people wish to acquire a working knowledge of economic and commercial terms for use in their daily life.

This encyclopaedia is designed to provide a useful, reliable and readable guide to the fast expanding field of economics and commerce. It contains a careful selection of key terms and concepts in economics and commerce which are considered important for a cross-section of readers including teachers and students of economics, commerce, law and management. This valuable reference work will also be useful for bankers, corporate executives, legislators and government officials. Entries on more technical terms are brief. However, topics of general interest have been explained in the form of essays rather than mere definitions. Both beginners and seasoned professionals will find it full of indispensable facts.

Meticulously cross-referenced, the encyclopaedia is a comprehensive and invaluable source of essential information. Though adequate care has been taken to include in the encyclopaedia as many terms and concepts as possible, a few omissions are likely in this kind of endeavour. The publisher will feel obliged to be informed of such omissions that could find place in the next edition. Similarly, suggestions are welcome to improve the completeness and accuracy of the terms explained in the encyclopaedia.

Thanks are due to the members of the editorial team who all worked tirelessly with their expertise to prepare this encyclopaedia.

Using the Encyclopaedia

The entries in the encyclopaedia are arranged in strict alphabetical order, letter by letter. A complete list of entries is given at the beginning of both the volumes of the encyclopaedia. To make the best use of the material included in the encyclopaedia and also to avoid repetition, entries are elaborately and meticulously cross-referenced in the following manner.

1. Cross-references immediately following an entry either indicate interchangeable terms, e.g. **Floating Debt See Ways and Means Advances** or direct the reader to the relevant description where that particular term is treated as part of a larger entry, e.g. **Open Market Operations See Central Bank**

2. Cross-references at the end of an entry point to the treatment of a related subject explained elsewhere in the encyclopaedia, e.g. **Monopsony:** It is a market situation where there is only one buyer but the number of sellers is very large. See also **Monopoly**.

3. Terms which appear during description of another term and are followed by (q.v.) are entered separately at relevant places in the encyclopaedia, e.g. **Cash Basis Accounting:** Under cash basis accounting, as against **Accrual Basis Accounting** (q.v.), a record is kept of actual receipts (cash incomings) and actual payments (cash outgoings) of a particular year.

An abbreviation is explained in full on its first appearance in each entry.

List of Entries

Volume I

A

D

Volume II

A

AAA Credit Rating

It is a rating classification in respect of credit worthiness of companies, public institutions and countries. AAA symbol indicates highest degree of commercial integrity with minimal risk of default. Other credit ratings in descending order of commercial integrity are: AA, A, BBB, BB, B etc. These ratings are awarded by Standard and Poor's or by Moody's, the two main rating companies of USA.

Ability-to-Pay Principle of Taxation

It states that if a given amount of revenue is needed to finance public services, then each taxpayer should contribute in line with his ability-to-pay taxes. Those who possess more economic power (income and wealth) should contribute more to public exchequer and vice versa. The duty to pay taxes is seen as a collective responsibility rather than a personal one. The ability-to-pay principle views tax policy issues in isolation to incidence of public expenditure. This principle is regarded by many as the most equitable and just method of taxation. It is emphasised primarily for its redistributive role.

For implementing the ability-to-pay rule, it is necessary to know as to how this ability is to be measured. Should ability-to-pay of an individual be identified with his income, net wealth, family size, health status of family members or some combination of these and other factors? And if a combination is to be considered, how to decide the relative weightage to be assigned to each of the various factors?

Formidable problems arise when two individuals with equal incomes but unequal wealth or equal wealth but unequal incomes are considered. More serious problems arise when individuals A and B have unequal incomes and unequal wealth in such a way that A has more income than B and B has more wealth than A. How is the inequality of income to be adjusted against the inequality of property? In short, the question is how should people with differing abilities be treated for the purpose of taxation?

Though not perfect, the index of taxable capacity is commonly interpreted in terms of a taxpayer's income with his wealth acting as a supplementary factor. Granted that ability-to-pay is to be measured in terms of income, it is simple that taxpayers with equal incomes should pay the same amount of tax. This is called *horizontal equity*, i.e. taxpayers in similar economic circumstances should bear the same tax burden, economic circumstances being defined in terms of level of income. The second aspect of ability-to-pay rule is *vertical equity*, i.e. taxpayers in dissimilar economic circumstances should bear dissimilar tax burden. Thus, persons earning more should pay more tax than those earning less. Obviously, formidable problems arise when taxpayers with different income levels are considered and decisions are required as to how the tax system should deal with these differences. In other words, how far taxes on people with different incomes should differ to ensure vertical equity?

Both the aspects of ability-to-pay rule are based on the philosophy that tax burden on individuals should be so distributed as to force them to make *equal sacrifice*, sacrifice being defined as loss of utility or satisfaction by surrendering units of money as tax.

Equal sacrifice rule, associated with such distinguished economists as J.S. Mill (1806-1873) and A.C. Pigou (1877-1959), is based on the following assumptions. 1. It is possible to relate units of income with units of utility. 2. The utility curve for income has a downward slope, i.e. marginal utility of income varies inversely with income. 3. The marginal utility of income curve is the same for all individuals.

Under these assumptions, the equal sacrifice rule is clear for taxpayers with equal incomes. They should surrender equal amounts as tax which in turn means sacrificing equal units of utility (horizontal equity). However, difficulties arise in interpreting equal sacrifice rule for people with different incomes. How is the term *equal* to be understood? In the tax literature the following three interpretations of the equal sacrifice rule are found.

1. Equal Absolute Sacrifice: It means the number of units of utility taken away from each taxpayer should be exactly the same.

2. Equal Proportional Sacrifice: Each taxpayer should be required to part with the same fraction of his total utility.

3. Equal Marginal Sacrifice: The marginal sacrifice is the same, i.e. utility left with, rather than taken from, every taxpayer after tax should be the same. This will ensure minimum total sacrifice for society, and hence it is also called *least aggregate sacrifice principle.*

Equal sacrifice theory is based on vague assumptions. Utility, being a psychological phenomenon, is not only non-measurable for any one individual but also non-comparable as between individuals. In short, determination of a tax base capable of measuring an individual's ability-to-pay is a major problem of tax theory. Yet this rule is incorporated in the form of progressive rate schedule for personal income tax, estate duty and property tax world-wide. See also Benefit Principle of Taxation.

Absolute Advantage, Theory of

It refers to a situation when out of two trading partner-countries, each one has an absolute cost advantage in producing a commodity (using similar and same quantities of resources) over the other. Suppose, there are two countries A and B both having only one factor of production (say labour) and producing two commodities X and Y. Country A produces 1 unit of commodity X with 5 units of labour and 1 unit of commodity Y with 3 units of labour while country B produces 1 unit of commodity X with 3 units of labour and 1 unit of Y with 4 units of labour. Then, it is said that country A has an absolute advantage in the production of commodity Y because 1 unit of its production requires 1 unit of labour less in it than in country B. Similarly, country B has an absolute advantage in the production of commodity X because 1 unit of it requires two units of labour less in it than in country A. This situation is considered to be the basis for territorial specialisation for the purpose of international trade. This view was propounded by Adam Smith (1723-1790) and later used by David Ricardo (1772-1823) in his theory of comparative cost.

Absolute Income Hypothesis See Consumption Function

Absorption Approach

It is an approach to understand the nature of and provide a remedy for a country's balance of payments deficit. Absorption here refers to the aggregate expenditure of a country, namely the sum total of consumption (C), investment (I) and government expenditure (G). If the absorption, i.e. aggregate expenditure (C+I+G) is more than that country's total output of goods and services, the gap is met by net imports and so there is a deficit in Balance of Payments (q.v.).

Under such a situation, exchange depreciation is generally recommended. However, it will be successful only if absorption also falls automatically or through government initiative.

Absorptive Capacity

It is a hypothesis maintaining that as the rate of investment in an economy increases, the productivity of new investment declines. Because of its implications as a constraint of growth, the term has relevance in development economics. In his *General Theory of Employment, Interest and Money* (1936), British economist J. M. Keynes (1883-1946) used the term *marginal efficiency of capital* for productivity of new investment and believed that it declines with the rate of new investment. The explanation offered is that as investment increases, less and less suitable equipment is employed in the production process.

Abstinence

In economics, payment of interest on money lent is justified as a reward for choosing to abstain from consumption for a specified period of time.

Accelerated Depreciation

It is a method under which entrepreneurs are allowed during the first year or the first few years after acquiring business assets to have depreciation allowances on a basis which exceeds the actual depreciation. This system provides incentive for capital investment by reducing the tax payable in the early years of the life of the assets concerned.

Acceleration Principle

It states that level of investment in an economy depends on the rate of change of national income.

Acceptance Credit

It is a short-term financing facility under which the borrower draws bills of exchange on a bank which accepts them and discounts them in the market to provide cash for the borrower.

Accession Tax

A donee-based tax on inheritances and gifts received. Accession tax was introduced in Japan in 1950 following the recommendations of Shoup Mission (q.v.).

Accrual Basis Accounting

There are two main methods of accounting: accrual basis accounting and Cash Basis Accounting (q.v.).

Under the accrual method (also called mercantile method), income tax is calculated with reference to income earned and sales made during the taxable period. Net profit/loss of a business is calculated by taking into account income and expenditure of a particular accounting year, irrespective of the fact whether such income is received or not, and expenditure is actually incurred or not during the accounting period.

Thus, income of a business accrued during the Previous Year (q.v.) is taxable whether it is received during the previous year or in a year following the previous year. Similarly, expenditure relating to previous year is deductible even if it is not incurred in the previous year.

Accrued Income

It is the income earned during a particular accounting period but not actually received during that period.

Accumulated Depreciation

It is the total depreciation expense accrued from the date of purchase of an asset to the present.

Across the Board Tariff Negotiations

These are negotiations involving uniform percentage reduction or increase in duty on major categories of items. The opposite is item-by-item tariff negotiations.

Activity Analysis

Economic situations frequently call for optimising a function subject to several inequality constraints. Activity analysis of production (also called *linear programming*) is concerned with the *set* of production processes available in a given economy. This set is called a production (possibility) set and any element or process or activity in this set describes the technological relation of an input with output. The objective is to determine the optimal allocation of scarce resources among competing products.

Actual Earning See Rent

Actuary

Actuary is a person trained in the calculation of risk and premiums for assurance purposes.

The primary function of an actuary is to monitor the financial position of the company on a sustained basis. He or she is supposed to continuously investigate the matters such as adequacy of reserves to meet the liabilities, the level to which solvency margin requirements are met, the investment policy of the company, the new products being introduced and their price etc. Based upon these investigations, the actuary is supposed to keep informed the management and directors of the company and also to the regulator on a continuous basis. In some of the countries, the actuary may even directly report to the regulator. The management of the company is supposed to take corrective measures as recommended by the actuary, if so required.

Additional Resource Mobilisation (ARM)

It means resources raised through additional efforts such as raising the rates of existing taxes and/or levying new taxes.

Adjustable Peg Exchange Rate

It is also known as IMF system or the gold exchange system. It avoids the rigidities of gold standard. It is adjustable and not chaotically fluctuating, i.e. it is pegged. Hence, the term *adjustable peg*. Exchange rates can vary by one per cent. Both ± fluctuations are allowed.

Member countries of IMF can adjust exchange rate only if there is a fundamental disequilibrium in the balance of payments.

Administered Prices

These are prices set consciously by a government rather than being determined by the free play of market forces. Prices of petroleum products in India are a case in point.

Administrative Costs

These are costs incurred by public authorities in administering a tax. These costs (also called expense ratio) include wages of tax officials and expenditure on stores and supplies for running tax administration. See also Cost-Yield Ratio.

***Ad Valorem* Duty**

A custom duty, an excise levy or a sales tax may be imposed either on *ad valorem* (according to value) basis or on specific basis. An *ad valorem* duty is imposed as a fixed percentage of the price of the product taxed. This form of duty is preferred when a commodity has many classifications and sub-classifications, e.g. textiles.

An *ad valorem* duty is responsive to price changes and thus ensures an undiminished proportion of taxes in national income. The main problem in applying *ad valorem* rate is the determination of the tax base, i.e. valuation of production.

An *ad valorem* duty may be a simple one, a duty collected as a fixed proportion of the price irrespective of the price range. As a variant of this, the commodity in question may be completely exempted till the price reaches a pre-determined maximum level. When different duty rates apply to different price brackets of a commodity, it becomes a graduated or bracketed *ad valorem* duty. So long as the price remains within a single bracket, the rate of the duty remains the same. Generally, commodities in higher price brackets bear a higher duty rate and vice versa. See also Specific Duty; and Compound Duty.

Advance Tax Payment

It is a system under which assessees are required to pay tax in advance on incomes which they expect to earn during the current financial year. Advance tax, payable in instalments during the financial year itself, is adjusted against the tax liability determined after proper assessment. Under Section 208 of the Indian Income Tax Act, 1961, it is obligatory to pay advance tax in every case where the advance tax payable is Rs. 5,000 or more. See also Withholding Tax.

African Development Bank

Set up in 1964 with headquarters at Abidjan, it has the chief function of providing development capital for African countries.

Against All Risks (AAR)

In marine insurance, this clause is added to cover the shipped goods with all risks of physical loss or damage.

Agents of Production See Factors of Production

Aid India Consortium

It was set up in 1956 to co-ordinate the assistance programmes of major donor countries for India.

Aid Tying See Foreign Aid

Airport Tax

It is levied as a lump sum per head at airports on departure of passengers.

Airway Bill

It is a consignment note issued by the airline carrying goods. It is not a document of title of goods.

Allowances

These are amounts the deductibility of which is statutorily allowed from the tax base, e.g. investment allowance. They have the effect of reducing the tax base.

Alternative Cost **See Opportunity Cost**

Alternative Minimum Tax **See Minimum Alternative Tax (MAT)**

Amortisation

In finance, it means the gradual repayment of a debt by means of a sinking fund. Thus, amortisation of debt means gradual reduction of a debt through periodic payments. In another context amortisation of an asset (machinery) refers to depreciation in its value over time.

Andean Group

Set up in 1969, it is an economic grouping comprising of six countries in the Andean subregion of Latin America, namely Chile, Bolivia, Columbia, Ecuador, Peru and Venezuela. Chile withdrew from the group in 1976. The Andean Group promotes regional economic integration and political co-operation among themselves.

Annual Value of House Property

It is deemed to be the sum for which a property might reasonably be expected to let from year to year. The annual value is ascertained by taking into consideration all relevant facts such as rent received, terms of the lease, municipal valuation, rent paid for similar property in the locality and so on. From the annual value of house property, various deductions are allowed in computing the net annual value of house property. These deductions pertain to municipal taxes, repairs of the property etc.

Annuity

It is a fixed sum of money paid to an annuitant yearly, usually for the remaining part of his life. It is a form of pension which provides a regular annual income. An annuity may be purchased by making a lump sum cash payment.

Antagonistic Mode of Production See Mode of Production

Anti-dumping Tariff

It is imposed to discourage dumping. The tariff rate is usually the difference between the normal selling price and the dumping price. Dumping means the sale of a product in a foreign market at a price much below that at which it is being sold in the domestic market.

Anti-trust Policy

It prohibits monopoly, restraints of trade and other practices to inhibit competition. Although many countries have adopted anti-trust legislations, USA was the first to do so when the Federal law, the Sherman Antitrust Act, 1890 outlawed monopolies and restraints of trade. This Act was revised and strengthened by another Federal statute, namely Clayton Antitrust Act enacted in 1914. In India, anti-trust policy is pursued through the Monopolies and Restrictive Trade Practices Act, 1968.

Appreciation of Currency

It refers to gradual increase in the external value of a currency in a free and fluctuating exchange market over several days/weeks. The increase is generally due to favourable supply and demand factors and without any specific or deliberate attempt made by monetary authorities to do so.

Arab Fund for Economic and Social Development (AFESD)

AFESD is an Arab regional financial organisation with an independent juridical status. Its membership includes all Arab countries that are members of the League of Arab States. Economic Council of the League of Arab States approved the Agreement establishing the Arab Fund on 16 May 1968.

The Agreement became effective on December 18, 1971. The first meeting of the Board of Governors was convened on February 6, 1972. The Fund commenced its operations at the beginning of 1974.

The Fund assists economic and social development of Arab countries through: (a) financing of development projects, with preference given to overall Arab development and joint Arab projects, (b) encouraging investment of private and public funds in Arab projects and (c) providing technical assistance services for Arab economic and social development.

Arbitrage

It is a term used in the context of international short-term capital flows. It refers to profiting by buying some financial asset/currency at a lower price and selling at a higher price in two different markets when both prices are known to the trader. So, there is no risk involved in it. For example, if dollar is cheaper in Kuwait than in Singapore, arbitrageurs will buy it in Kuwait and sell in Singapore. This will continue till the two rates are equal.

If the exchange rates in various centres (more than two) are made mutually consistent, it is called *triangular arbitrage.*

Arm's Length Price

It is the market price that would have been negotiated by unrelated parties engaged in similar transactions under similar conditions. Arm's length standard is used to prevent the use of Transfer Pricing (q.v.) technique for tax avoidance. Many countries exercise their right to adjust reported transfer prices to conform to arm's length criterion. However, implementing the arm's length principle has proved to be a difficult task for tax authorities.

Array

An array is an arrangement of raw numerical data in ascending or descending order of magnitude. The difference between the largest and smallest numbers is called the *range* of the data.

Asian Currency Market

On the pattern of Euro currency market, this market operating in Singapore deals in buying and selling of international currencies like dollar, mark and pound.

Asian Development Bank (ADB)

This multilateral development finance institution is engaged in promoting economic and social progress of its developing member countries in the Asian and Pacific region. Its headquarters are in Manila, Philippines.

The Bank began its operations in December 1966. It is owned by the governments of 40 countries from the region and 16 countries from outside the region. Over the years, the Bank has been a catalyst in promoting the development of the most populous region in the world. It provides technical assistance for the preparation and execution of development projects and programmes. It promotes investment of public and private capital for development purposes. The Bank gives special attention to the needs of the smaller and less developed countries. It gives priority to regional, subregional, and national projects and programmes which contribute to the harmonious economic growth of the region as a whole and which promote regional co-operation.

The Bank's ordinary capital resources consist of subscribed capital and reserves and funds raised through borrowings. It also has special funds made up of contributions from member countries, accumulated net income, and amounts previously set aside from paid-in capital.

The Bank borrows funds for its ordinary operations from the capital markets of the world and from central banks of certain member countries. The Bank's callable capital, which at the end of 1996 accounted for 93 per cent of its subscribed capital, backs its borrowings in the capital markets.

The Bank's operations cover a wide spectrum of socio-economic activities. Its medium-term strategic objectives are to foster economic growth, reduce poverty, improve the status of women, support human development (including population planning) and protect the environment.

Board of Governors is the highest policymaking body of the Bank which meets annually. Board of Directors, composed of 12 Directors (8 representing regional countries and 4 nonregional countries) is responsible for general operations of the Bank. The Board of Governors elects the Board of Directors every two years.

The President of the Bank is elected by the Board of Governors for a term of 5 years. The President is responsible for the organisation, appointment and dismissal of officers and staff in accordance with regulations adopted by the Board of Directors.

The Bank has 23 departments and offices at its headquarters. It also has 7 Resident Missions: Dhaka (Bangladesh), Phnom Penh (Cambodia), New Delhi (India), Jakarta (Indonesia), Kathmandu (Nepal), Islamabad (Pakistan), and Hanoi (Vietnam); a South Pacific Regional Mission in Port Vila (Vanuatu); and three Representative offices, one each in Tokyo (Japan), Frankfurt (Germany) for Europe, and Washington (USA) for North America. Resident Missions are also being opened in Almaty (Kazakhistan and Uzbekistan) and Colombo (Sri Lanka). At the end of 1996, the Bank had 653 professional staff and 1,286 supporting staff.

Member Countries of ADB With Year of Membership

Country	Year
Regional	
Afghanistan	1966
Australia	1966
Bangladesh	1973
Bhutan	1982
Cambodia	1966
China, People's Republic of	1986
Cook Islands	1976
Fiji	1970
Hong Kong, China	1969
India	1966
Indonesia	1966
Japan	1966
Kazakhistan	1994
Kiribati	1974
Korea, Republic of	1966
Kyrgyz Republic	1994
Non-Regional	
Austria	1966
Belgium	1966
Canada	1966
Denmark	1966
Finland	1966
France	1970
Germany	1966
Italy	1966
The Netherlands	1966
Norway	1966
Spain	1986
Sweden	1966
Switzerland	1967
Turkey	1991
UK	1966
USA	1966

Assessee

An assessee is a person by whom a tax is payable under some tax law. It includes every person in respect of whom any proceeding has been taken up for the assessment of his income, wealth, etc. It also includes a person who is assessable in respect of income of another person.

Asset

Ownership of any physical property or right that has money value is called asset. Land, buildings, machinery and other forms of physical property are called *tangible assets*. Goodwill, patents, trademarks, copyrights and other non-material benefits are called *intangible assets*. Similarly, cash in hand, marketable securities, inventories and other assets which can be readily converted into money are called *current assets* while plant, equipment and time deposits are *fixed assets* because they are not readily convertible into money.

Assignment of Tax

Assignment of a tax means transfer of taxation power from a higher level to a lower level government. Taxation power includes the following: right to levy the tax, collect the tax, and appropriate the proceeds from the tax.

Generally, the purpose of tax assignment is to augment the resources of lower level governments. The assignment of tax may be conditional. Thus, it may be obligatory on the part of a lower level government to levy the tax assigned to it. Not only this, the lower level government may not have powers to alter the basic structure of the assigned tax. It may enjoy flexibility in fixing the tax rates within a minimum and maximum range prescribed by the higher level government.

Assignment Rules of Foreign Income See Double Taxation

Association See Correlation

Association of South-East Asian Nations (ASEAN)

It comprises of Brunei Darssalam, Indonesia, Laos, Malaysia, Myanmar, Philippines, Singapore, Thailand and Vietnam.

Atlantic Charter

It was an understanding between USA and UK reached during World War II for giving expression to their trade policies.

Attribute See Variable

Autarky

It is a self-sufficient, self-dependent, closed economy. It is free of any economic relations with the rest of the world. By definition, it rules out foreign trade.

Automatic Stabiliser

An automatic stabiliser (or built-in stabiliser) is one that works on its own accord, without requiring deliberate action on the part of public authorities. Most such stabilisers are fiscal in nature, e.g. personal and corporate income taxes levied with a progressive rate schedule. These taxes rise and fall with personal and business incomes. A galloping economy is slowed down through higher taxes while a sagging economy is stimulated through lower taxes.

Availability Hypothesis

According to Irving B. Kravis, a country imports those items which are *not available at home* or can be produced only at a much higher cost due to lack of natural resources, supply rigidities and high transport cost. Conversely, a country exports those items which are *available*. Availability here means an elastic supply made possible by sufficiency of resources, innovations and favourable tariff policy. Thus, a country's commodity-composition of trade is explained by *availability*.

Average Cost See Cost of Production

Average Propensity to Import

It is the fraction of total national income that is spent on imports, measured as a ratio of total imports to total domestic expenditure.

Average Revenue See Revenue

Average Tax Rate

It is derived by expressing tax amount as a percentage of taxable income. It is also called effective tax rate.

Averaging of Income See Income Averaging

B

Backward-bending Supply Curve of Labour

Supply of labour depends on three factors: (a) size of the population, (b) proportion of working population and (c) number of hours worked by each worker.

Number of hours worked by each worker bears close relationship with the wage rate. A worker has 24 hours at his disposal per day. He divides these hours between work (earning) and leisure. If there is an increase in wage rate, it induces him to work for more hours. Leisure becomes costlier after the wage hike. Hence, there is a kind of substitution effect in favour of work and against leisure. However, increase in wage rate makes him better off in terms of income and he can afford to have more leisure. Thus, substitution effect and income effect move in opposite directions and his decision to have more (or less) leisure would depend on their relative strength. If the substitution effect is stronger than the income effect, he will have less leisure (i.e. more work). Conversely, if income effect is stronger than substitution effect, he will have more leisure (i.e. less work).

Thus, the shape of the supply curve of labour depends on the relative strength of the substitution effect and income effect. In the Figure below when the wage rate is W_1, the number of hours worked is zero. As the wage rate rises from W_1 to W_2, more and more hours are worked and the supply curve of labour has a positive slope. When the wage rate rises above W_2, the number of hours worked falls so that the supply curve has a negative slope. This situation creates the famous backward-sloping supply curve of labour. See also Wages.

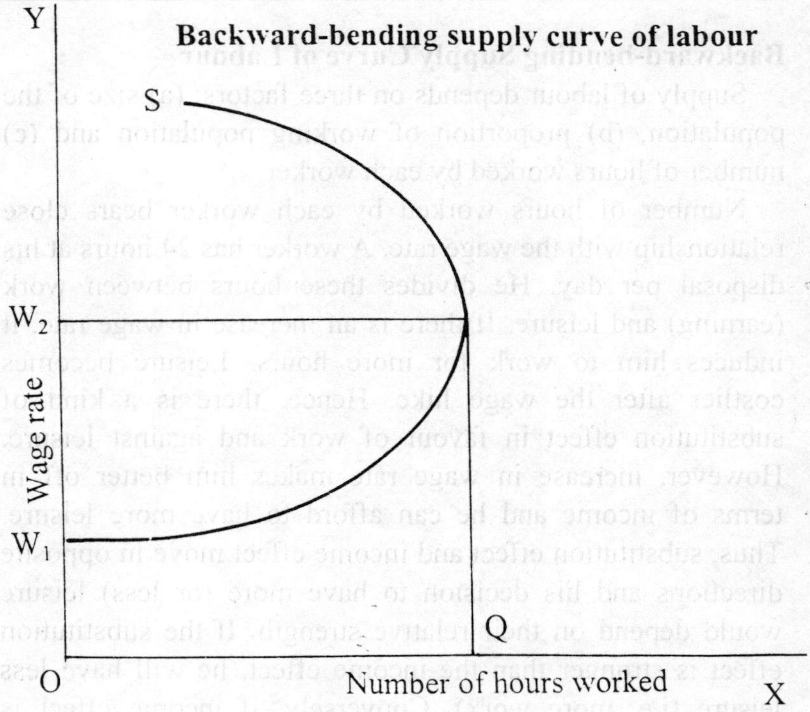

Backward Shifting See Shifting of Tax

Bad Debt

It is a loan which is not likely to be repaid due to borrower's insolvency or dishonesty.

Balanced Budget

It is a situation in which current revenue of the government is exactly equal to its current expenditure.

Balanced Budget Multiplier

It measures the change in national income divided by the balanced-budget change in government expenditure. For example, if an extra Rs. 10 crore of government expenditure, financed by an extra Rs. 10 crore of taxes, causes national income to rise by Rs. 5 crore, the balanced-budget multiplier is 0.5.

Balanced Growth

The term refers to a strategy of planned and co-ordinated development of all the sectors of an economy. The underlying philosophy of this development strategy (usually recommended for less developed countries) is to minimise the occurrence of shortages and overproduction in different sectors of an economy.

Balance of International Indebtedness

It is a statement of the net claims of the residents of a country against the residents of the rest of the world. Also known as *international investment position* or b*alance sheet for the foreign sector,* it is derived from all debits and credits in the capital account of a country's balance of payments measured at the prevailing exchange rate. From this, one can know a country's net credit or net debit position. It also reflects the liquidity position of a country, i.e. how does the maturity structure of assets compare with the maturity structure of liabilities. If assets are mainly long- term and liabilities short-term, there can be a liquidity problem for the country.

Balance of Payments

Political and geographical boundaries of the world do not coincide with the natural resources, skills and other essentials for the betterment of human welfare. World trade and financial flows reflect sharp variances in needs and advantages among individual countries. At any given time some nations will show surpluses in trade and payment balances while others will experience corresponding deficits.

Balance of payments is a financial statement of a country showing the flows of goods, services and funds between its residents and those of rest of the world during a given period of time. It is based on double entry book-keeping system.

The process through which the authorities correct the balance of payments imbalance includes exchange rate variations, changes in government expenditure, checking imports/capital flows, inducing changes in economic structure and removing distortions and undesirable pressures.

Book Keeping in Balance of Payments: It is maintained in double entry book keeping form. In principle, each transaction gives rise to two entries, one on the credit side and another on the debit side. Total of the two sides are always equal. Hence, balance of payments is always in balance. For example, import is recorded as a debit item. However, an offsetting entry on credit side of equal amount is also made by reducing importer's holding of foreign currency and increasing other's holding of this currency on account payable.

Monetary Theory/Monetarist Approach in Balance of Payments: It explains the deficit in balance of payments in terms of excess supply of money. According to this theory, excess supply of money in an open economy can be eliminated by a balance of payments deficit which would continue until the difference between supply of and demand for money is eliminated.

With fixed exchange rate, balance of payments deficit means that the economy is adjusting to excess supply of money which authorities have created. With flexible exchange rate, domestic economy is insulated from foreign monetary developments. Then the economy adjusts to an excess supply of money through rise in domestic prices and fall in exports leading to fall in exchange rate. Exchange rate falls till original differential between domestic and foreign price levels is restored.

Neo-Cambridge Approach to Balance of Payments: It relates balance of payments to the public sector financial deficit on the assumption that private sector financial surplus is broadly constant over time. Assuming constancy of private sector surplus, variations in balance of payments must be broadly equal to (and opposite to) variations in public sector financial deficit via conventional accounting identities. Moreover, since exports depend on exchange rate and changes in balance of payments are through changes in public sector financial deficit, the main role of exchange rate is to determine the level of domestic economic activity and volume of employment. This approach assumes marginal propensity to save being equal to zero and it is the marginal propensity to import which is the only leakage for the domestic economy.

Structural Approach to Balance of Payments: According to this approach, balance of payments is determined through the entire structure of the economy. It considers traded and non-traded goods, elasticities of demand and supply, income-expenditure mechanism and Keynesian foreign trade multiplier. Real expenditure decisions depend on wealth, monetary factors, expectations etc. and the essential role of balance of payments is to explain variations in private sector surplus.

Structural Maladjustment: A country's industrial structure may simply be in poor adjustment with the world pattern of wants. It may continue to produce those goods which are no longer in demand and fail to produce those items which are in demand. Hence, exports alone may be causing balance of payments disequilibrium which can be checked only by making structural adjustments, i.e. changing the composition of national output by reallocating factors of production as per demand from other countries. This is done by changing relative prices, bringing fiscal measures like tariff or subsidies to help growth of new industries. Structural maladjustment, if not corrected in time, can lead to disequilibrium, leading to cut in imports and consequent fall in standard of living. Mere exchange controls tend to postpone the problem. Hence, structural adjustments or changes in the composition of national output through resource reallocation are the only way to solve balance of payments disequilibrium.

Balance of Trade

It is the difference between merchandise exports and imports of a country. It is the most important category in balance of payments. Since data on exports and imports are available sooner than on other items, it shows the trends of balance of payments quite early.

Balance Sheet

Balance sheet of a business entity (e.g. a bank) is a statement of its liabilities and assets at a point of time. It reflects the policies, size and soundness of the operations of the business. The liabilities indicate the sources of its funds. The assets show the nature of its investments. For example, the liabilities of a bank include paid-up capital and reserves, deposits, borrowings and bills payable. Similarly, assets of a bank include, *inter alia*, cash in hand, money at call/short notice, investment in securities and loans and advances.

Bank for International Settlements (BIS)

This bank was set up at the Hague Conference in January 1930 to help in the collection of German reparation payments. It consisted of Belgium, France, Germany, Italy, Japan, UK and USA. Later on it acted as a clearing office for European Payments Union (EPU), i.e. to keep records of inter-country debit/credit entries of each EPU member-country with non-EPU countries.

The BIS has always been a central banking institution which is unique at the international level. It is owned and controlled by central banks and it provides a number of highly-specialised services to central banks and through them to the international financial system more generally. At present, BIS is actively deepening its relationships with central banks outside its traditional focus in the industrialised world.

The BIS commenced its activities in Basle on 17th May 1930 and is thus the world's oldest international financial organisation. Presently, Basle has become the traditional international meeting place for many central bank governors and other officials.

Bank Rate Policy **See Central Bank**

Barriers to Trade

Barriers to trade are obstacles which prevent goods and services from moving freely between nations on the basis of pure competition and comparative advantage. They are interferences imposed by national governments as part of trade policy in pursuit of such goals as a balanced international payments position, internal economic development, protection for an important domestic industry and maintenance of indigenous productive capacity in a strategic area.

Though tariff barriers continue to be important in modern day trade policy, the non-tariff barriers have captured most of the attention in the last few decades. In addition to quotas, some of the more prominent non-tariff barriers are multiple (discriminatory) exchange rate systems, countervailing duties, orderly marketing agreements (voluntary export quotas), multiple valuation procedures for purposes of levying tariffs on imports, administrative hindrances in processing of import goods, technical standards and specifications ill-suited to foreign goods, and discriminatory government procurement practices. These barriers represent a diverse collection of protectionist devices used by governments to influence trade patterns.

Barter

It is a system in which goods are traded directly for other goods. The main problem of barter system is double coincidence of wants which means each of the two parties seeks to obtain the commodity that it desires and that the other party must possess it.

Base Currency

It is the currency against which the exchange rate of another currency is determined. For example, if rupee is quoted as Rs. 43 = 1 US $, then dollar is the base currency. Rupee is the quoted currency.

Basic Economic Activities

The three basic economic activities are: Production (q.v.), Consumption (q.v.) and Capital formation (q.v.).

Basic Features of an Economy

All economies of the world are characterised by three basic features which cause all economic problems.

Resources are Limited: Resources like land, minerals and skilled workers are limited in every country. It is true that some economies have more resources than others but there is always a limit to the availability of resources in every country. Since the resources are limited, the capacity of every economy to produce goods and services is also limited.

Wants are Unlimited: Human wants everywhere are unlimited and insatiable. Even in rich countries of the world, there is no end to the demand for goods and services. Human wants arise again and again and multiply with the advancement of society.

Resources Have Alternative Uses: Most economic resources can be put to various uses. For example, a hectare of land can be used for growing wheat or as a playground or as a garden and so on. However, it cannot be used for all these purposes simultaneously. Most economic problems arise because of this feature of resources.

Basic Personal Exemption

Income tax laws of almost all countries conventionally grant exemption of a given portion of income which does not reflect taxpaying capacity of a person. There are two considerations for this exemption. 1. Tax bite into income, barely sufficient for a minimum standard of living, is immoral. 2. It is administratively difficult to deal with low income earners.

What should be the level of basic personal exemption? It is a value-laden issue without a straightforward answer. The cut-off point for initial deduction as a multiple of per capita income varies from country to country.

Basic Problems of an Economy

Every country is faced with a host of economic problems. Some of these problems are specific to the country concerned. However, there are three economic problems which are common to all economies of the world. Since every country has to face these problems, they are called central (or basic or fundamental) problems of an economy. These problems were there in olden days, are present in modern times and will be faced in the future also. These problems which arise in a given sequence are the following:

Resource Allocation: Since resources are scarce, it is not possible for a country to produce as much of every commodity as desired by its citizens. For example, if more land is devoted to the cultivation of wheat, less would be available for growing sugarcane. Similarly, if more steel is used for construction of buildings, less would be available for railways. In short, more of one commodity usually means less of others. Therefore, every economy must decide which goods to produce and in what quantity. This is the problem of resource allocation.

Choice of Technology: The second problem pertains to choosing an appropriate technology for the production of various goods and services. It is well-known that most commodities can be produced using different combinations of factors of production. For example, we can produce cloth using a modern automatic textile machine or with the help of handlooms. Apparently, some techniques use more capital as compared to labour and are therefore called capital-intensive or labour-saving techniques of production. Conversely, certain other methods of production use more of labour than capital and are therefore called labour-intensive or capital-saving techniques of production. Every society must decide which type of technique it has to adopt in the production process. In other words, this problem relates to the ratio in which factors of production (land, labour and capital) are to be used in the production process.

Distribution: Since resources are scarce therefore the production of goods and services is limited. It is not possible to satisfy all the wants of all the people of a country. Thus, very few people get motor cars in a poor country while most others are left desiring it. There must be some mechanism to decide as to how many of the wants of each individual are to be satisfied. In other words, the society must evolve some method so that total production gets distributed among different individuals in a lawful manner. This is the problem of distribution of national income.

The three basic problems of an economy mentioned above are common to all types of economic system be it capitalism, socialism, or some other form of economic organisation. However, different economic systems solve these problems differently. Let us now examine how these problems are solved in (a) a capitalistic society, (b) a socialist society and (c) a mixed economy.

In a capitalist or a free enterprise economy, the means of production are owned by private individuals or groups of individuals (companies, partnership firms etc.). These means of production are used for maximising profit for the owners. Competition is another feature of a capitalist society. These characteristics of a capitalist society must be kept in mind to understand the solution of central problems in it.

Price mechanism is the instrument through which a capitalist society solves its central problems. Producers produce those goods for which consumers are willing to pay prices which, besides covering the cost of production, generate sufficient profit for them. Normally, an increase in the price of a commodity increases its supply and vice versa. Irrespective of the needs of the community, producers will produce those goods which bring them the maximum profit. Millions of producers act independently in taking production decisions without any central guidance. Still, only those goods are produced which the consumers want the most. This is the wonder of price mechanism.

The problem of choice of technology is also solved by the operation of prices, this time the prices of factors of production. Every producer tries to minimise his cost of production. For this purpose, he takes into account the price of labour (wage rate), price of capital services (interest rates) and so on. He will mix different factors of production in such a way that his per unit or average cost is minimised. He will use less of expensive factors of production and more of relatively cheap factors of production. For example, low wage rate of unskilled labour in India is primarily responsible for widespread adoption of labour-intensive technology. Thus, the second fundamental problem is also solved by price mechanism.

Solution of the third problem also lies in the price mechanism. The economy will produce commodities for those who have the money to pay for them. The higher the income of an individual, the more commodities he will get. Those who have less purchasing power will claim less share in national product. The purchasing power of an individual is determined by (a) the price of the commodity or service which he is offering in the market and (b) the prices of commodities and services which he is purchasing in the market. Thus, if the price of his commodity or service remains the same but prices of commodities purchased by him increase, then his share in national product will decrease.

Socialist or a centrally planned economy is an economic system totally different from a capitalist society. In a socialist economy, the means of production are owned by the state, i.e. all land, buildings, factories and machines and equipments are the property of the government. In other words, private property is prohibited. Means of production are used by the state for the general welfare of society. Government enjoys monopoly in the production and distribution of all goods and services. In such a society, prices of commodities and factors of production are fixed by the government. Therefore, price mechanism has no role to play and all decisions regarding production, choice of technology, and distribution are taken by government agencies such as the planning commission. On the basis of past records, the planning commission allocates resources for various uses in such a way that different commodities are produced according to their likely demand. If the actual demand for a commodity exceeds or falls short of the available supply, the administration will revise its production decision for the next year. In short, socialist society works on the basis of *trial and error method*. It is not a flexible system like a free enterprise economy.

Second problem (choice of technology) is also solved by administrative decisions. Unlike a capitalist society, wages are fixed by the government in a socialist society. Government agencies like planning commission take stock of the available factors of production. If the choice of a particular technology leaves part of the labour force unemployed then in the next round the authorities will opt for a more labour-intensive technique of production.

In a socialist society, the distribution of national income is more equitable. Since everybody is a wage earner therefore inequalities of income are modest. The basic philosophy of a socialist society is: from each according to his ability and to each according to his needs. Thus, government ensures equity and fairness in the distribution of available supplies of goods and services. In brief, the role of price mechanism is played by economic planning in a socialist society.

Solution of the central problems in a mixed economy is partly on the basis of price mechanism and partly through administrative decisions of the government. The private sector of a mixed economy behaves in the same way as a capitalist economy (maximising profit). Conversely, the public sector in a mixed economy is not always guided by the objective of profit maximisation. Many public enterprises are set up in backward areas to provide employment and income to the people of that region.

Similarly, the prices of public sector products are fixed by the government. Government also interferes in the working of the economy through fiscal and monetary measures and sometimes through physical controls like rationing.

Thus, every economy has to solve the central problems and various methods are adopted for this purpose.

Basket Valuation of SDRs

It is a group of five currencies (US dollar, Deutsche mark, Japanese yen, French franc and Pound sterling) represented proportionately on the basis of size of exports of these countries. It is used by International Monetary Fund to determine the value of Special Drawing Rights (SDRs).

Bastable Test

Named after Charles Francis Bastable (1855-1945), it advocates that an infant industry which is being given protection must guarantee that eventual gain to the economy from this industry will be sufficient to cover the losses (high cost of imports) it suffers during the infancy period.

Beggar-thy-neighbour Policy

A country suffering from depression or trade deficit may reduce its imports. Reduced imports mean fall in the exports of the trade partner and hence fall in its economic activities. Thus, the former country is said to have undertaken beggar-thy-neighbour policies. Its level of employment and income is enhanced at the cost of its neighbour (trade partner).

Benefit Principle of Taxation

According to this traditional approach, an equitable tax system is one under which tax payments are based on the amount of benefits received from government services. In other words, the cost of government services should be apportioned among individuals according to the relative benefits they enjoy. Clearly, implementation of the benefit principle presupposes determination of the incidence of public expenditure before deciding distribution of tax burden. Thus, it encompasses issues of both tax and expenditure policies.

Two objections are generally raised against the benefit principle of taxation, one on grounds of practicability and the other on considerations of desirability. For implementing the benefit principle, the beneficiaries of public expenditure must be identified. This may be possible in the case of highway tolls, fishing and hunting licences and property taxes. However, it is very difficult to allocate costs or benefits of the majority of government services among citizens. Who benefits from defence services, maintenance of foreign relations, space technology, or contributions to UNO? Costs of these services cannot be divided and assigned logically to the recipients of the benefits. Most services of modern governments are provided in the interest of group rather than individual welfare. These difficulties limit the practicability of the benefit theory.

Even if it is possible to identify persons or classes receiving direct benefit from government services, it may not be desirable to tax them accordingly. This is particularly so in underdeveloped countries where tax policy is used as a tool of distributive justice. Governments in these countries have launched ambitious programmes, financed mainly through taxes, to solve the twin problems of unemployment and poverty. These welfare-oriented schemes include subsidised/free medical and educational facilities, low-cost housing, drinking water facilities in rural areas, land improvement schemes, and employment guarantee programmes. The beneficiaries of these schemes are not expected to compensate the government for the benefits received. Similarly, certain transfer payments (like scholarships to needy students or outright money grants to widows or handicapped) are financed from taxes and it would be ridiculous to expect the beneficiaries to contribute to public exchequer in line with the benefits received.

In short, tax policy is also an instrument of social change and not merely a charge for the services rendered by public bodies. The redistributive role of tax policy cannot be realised through benefit approach which is based on the implicit assumption of equitable distribution of economic power. Hence, the application of benefit theory of taxation is not widespread in the modern world. See also Ability-to-Pay Principle of Taxation.

Benelux

It is a customs union of Belgium, the Netherlands and Luxembourg formed in 1948.

Bentham's Criterion See Welfare Economics

Bergson Social Welfare Function See Welfare Economics

Best Judgement Assessment

It is an assessment made by a tax officer against a person who is in default of furnishing information as regards his income, wealth etc. Thus, where an assessee fails to file a return or submit documents called for or comply with the terms of a notice, the assessing officer may assess total income, wealth etc. according to the best of his judgement. This he can do after giving the assessee an opportunity of being heard.

Betterment Levy

It is a tax on unearned increment in connection with town improvement (betterment) schemes. Execution of a development scheme by public authorities generally leads to increase in the annual and capital value of land and buildings under the scope of the scheme. Such appreciation is not the result of any individual efforts, but materialises from the corporate activity of the community as a whole. Betterment levy on unearned increment in land values is justified on the ground that it provides additional resources to the government to liquidate partially or fully the capital cost of the development scheme.

Betting Tax

It is levied on horse races. The tax is levied on stakeholder who may be either a race club or a bookmaker. The law governing betting tax is generally regulatory in nature. The main objective is to discourage poorer sections of the population from gambling on horse races.

Biased Integration

It refers to economic integration involving reduction/elimination of barriers to trade or to factor mobility between a group of countries but not between them and the rest of the world. See also Customs Union.

Big Mac Index

Big Mac stands for McDonalds chain of world-wide fast food centres. The price it charges for its hamburger sandwiches in different countries is used to measure purchasing power parity index. For example, if hamburger costs $ 2 in USA and 400 Yen in Japan, then the equilibrium exchange rate between dollar and yen is $ 2 = 400 yen or $ 1 = 200 yen. But if the official exchange rate is $ 1 = 180 yen then yen can be considered to be an over-valued currency.

The Economist magazine publishes Big Mac Updates each year.

Bilateral Aid See Foreign Aid

Bilateral Double Tax Conventions See Double Tax Treaty

Bilateral Monopoly

It is a market situation in which there is only one seller and one buyer of a product/service. Thus, the owner of a sugar mill located in a remote area may be the only buyer of the services of labour and if the local workers negotiate with him collectively through their trade union, a situation of bilateral monopoly will emerge.

Bilateral Trade Agreement

It refers to trade agreement separately done between two countries on various trade issues like its volume, composition, mode of payments etc. or for balancing their mutual payments.

Bill of Lading

It is a document issued by the shipping company as a receipt for goods shipped and also as an undertaking that these will be delivered to the consignee.

Bimetallism

It refers to the policy under which the value of the monetary unit of a country is defined in terms of two different metals (generally gold and silver) by setting the ratio of the coined value of one metal to the other.

Birth-rate

It is defined as the number of births per thousand of population in a country during a year. In demography, it is termed as crude birth rate.

Black Market

It is the unauthorised/illegal segment of the market in which goods are sold at prices that violate the legal restrictions on prices.

Black Money

The term black money stands for money earned by illegal means and kept secretly and unaccounted for. It is widely used for smuggling activities, hoarding of scarce commodities (for purposes of speculation, profiteering and black marketing), bribing government officials, financing political activities, and ostentatious living. Secret business deals through black money in turn lead to tax evasion and a vicious circle is created in which one evil thrives on the other.

Blue Chip

The term refers to the shares of a large reputed company whose earnings and dividend records have been stable or growing over the years. Blue chip shares are generally priced high in relation to a company's earnings due to its good reputation.

Bond

A bond is a promise to pay a stated sum of money as interest each year and to repay the face value of bond at some future redemption date. Some bonds, called *perpetuities*, pay a fixed sum of interest each year forever but never repay the principal, i.e. they have no redemption date.

Bonded Warehouse

It is a warehouse licensed and bonded by the government to insure against loss of customs duty. Goods subject to customs duty may be stored there without paying duty. Such goods are said to be under bond. These storage facilities are operated under the lock and key of a country's customs authorities and the owners of these facilities are bonded to ensure that they will satisfy all customs duty obligations. The importer will have to pay the existing duty on the goods if they enter the domestic market. Sometimes, the stored goods are repacked or further processed there. But if additional domestic materials are used they are exempt from duty, only the import portion is subject to customs duty.

Bonus Issue

It refers to shares issued by a company to existing shareholders not in respect of the subscription of new capital but as a capitalisation of reserves. The extra shares are issued free on a pro rata basis. They may not by themselves confer any benefits to shareholders. They bring the issued capital more into line with the real capital of the company which may have appreciated in value in money terms.

Book Value

It is the cash value of machinery/capital goods of a company after deducting depreciation.

Boom

It is a period of high output and high employment in an economy.

Border Tax See Customs Duty

Bracket Creep

It is a situation when a person's income, rising at the same rate as price level, faces higher rates of taxation. See also Index-Linked Adjustment.

Brain Drain

It refers to the movement of highly trained personnel from the less developed countries (LDCs) to the developed West due to higher returns available there. This deprives the LDCs of their services and return on investment in skill formation. Hence, capital-in-disguise moves from the LDCs to the rich countries.

Break-even Point

It refers to that quantity of sales with which a firm neither makes profit nor incurs losses. Above this level, the firm starts earning profit, and below it, suffers losses. Breakeven point analysis is used to estimate profit/loss of a firm at various levels of output.

Bretton Woods Conference

This Conference of Allied Nations was held at Bretton Woods, New Hampshire, USA in July 1944. Forty four countries participated in it and resolved to establish International Monetary Fund (IMF) and the International Bank for Reconstruction and Development (IBRD). An agreement was signed to provide a stable monetary environment to facilitate the economic reconstruction of the world after World War II. The Conference itself was the outcome of lengthy trans-Atlantic negotiations. IMF was meant to symbolise a new international monetary system under which fixed exchange rate system (of nearly all principal currencies) was made the base.

Brussels Trade Classification

Before Standard International Trade Classification (SITC) was adopted in early 1950s, Brussels classification was in vogue. It had five main categories: (a) live animals, (b) food, (c) raw materials and semi-manufactures, (d) manufactures and (e) gold and silver.

Budget

It is a financial plan listing expenditure and income expected during some given future period, usually one year. A budget may be prepared by an individual, a family, a company, or a government.

Individuals and families expect income from salaries, interest-bearing securities, rent and gifts. They anticipate expenditure on food, clothing, housing, education, health care, entertainment etc. A company budget is usually based on expected output and sale proceeds, and anticipated expenses. A government budget is based on expected tax and non-tax revenues, and expenditure on defence, external affairs, educational institutions, hospitals, and a host of other administrative, developmental and maintenance activities.

When income and expenditure are equal over some period of time, the budget is said to be balanced. In practice, even the most carefully planned budgets result in excess of income over expenditure (surplus budget) or excess of expenditure over income (deficit budget).

Public Versus Private Budgeting: Neither a government nor an individual can function without finance. Individuals and governments both have sources of receipts and heads of expenditure and face the problem of adjustment between the two. Both the entities try to maximise welfare with limited means. Despite these few points of similarities, public budgeting is altogether a different exercise as compared to private budgeting.

Individuals, unlike governments, may at their own risk earn and spend without planning, foresight and proper recording of their transactions. Governments in democracies are answerable for their actions to the legislators who in turn enjoy the mandate of the electorate. A private individual may prefer to keep his financial transactions a secret whereas financial activities of the government get wide publicity and are subject to audit and inspection.

Financial resources at the disposal of individuals are far less than available to a government. Like a government, a private organisation cannot impose taxes nor can it print currency. An individual regards surplus budget as a virtue and a means to accumulate capital to become rich. Contrarily, deficit budgeting is more a rule than exception for the government. Public authorities first determine the volume of expenditure and then arrange resources to meet it. In most cases, public expenditure is inelastic and has to be incurred, e.g. on defence, law and order and general administration.

Private budget-making is guided exclusively by profit motive while public budgeting has social welfare as the objective function. While performance of all private activities is capable of measurement with the standard of money, most public activities defy such measurement. In the absence of market mechanism, government services are determined not by profit expectations but by decisions arrived through political and administrative procedures and based on common social objectives.

Significance of Government Budgeting: Budgetary operations of a government have important bearing on the functioning of an economy. Government collects huge sums of money through taxes, borrowings and sale of treasury bills to the central bank. The manner of collecting and spending government funds greatly influences saving and investment levels, distribution of income and wealth, allocation of resources and consumption behaviour of the people.

Budget is not merely an exercise in matching expenditure to income. Rather, it is a powerful medium to realise objectives of public policy. A budget is a description of both the fiscal policies of the government and the financial plans corresponding to them.

It is necessary for governments to have planned appraisals of their earnings and proper means of controlling the channels of spending them. The absence of such exercises may lead to corruption, inefficiency and even bankruptcy. Hence, planned earning and wise spending are prerequisites for the stability of a government. Budget is the medium for fulfilling these requirements. Public budgeting is desirable from government's point of view because it can answer its critics squarely and prove its honesty in financial matters. It is also important for the legislators because they can ensure that all is well with the public money.

Revenue Budget Versus Capital Budget: In most countries, budget of the government is presented in two parts: revenue budget and capital budget.

Revenue budget shows revenue receipts of the government and the expenditures met from them. Thus, it consists of (a) revenue receipts and (b) revenue expenditure. All those receipts of the government which are non-redeemable may be termed as revenue receipts. These receipts are divided into (i) tax revenues and (ii) non-tax revenues.

Revenue expenditure relates to the normal running of government departments, interest charges on debt incurred by the government, grants given to state governments and other parties. Broadly speaking, all those expenditures of the government which do not result in the creation of physical or financial assets may be treated as revenue expenditures.

Capital budget shows capital requirements of the government and their financing pattern. Among the principal sources of meeting these requirements are: revenue surplus, regular floatation of loans in the domestic market, small savings and external borrowings. To the extent that these receipts fall short of the capital requirements, the deficit is made good by the issue of treasury bills and drawing down of cash balances. Capital account signifies that economic role of the government extends far beyond collecting and spending tax revenue. It reflects the influence of government over the economy through its acquisition and disposition of a significant portion of the annual savings of the people. The amount of savings available to the private sector for investment is reduced by the amount of capital raised by public authorities for development and public purposes.

Capital budget comprises capital receipts and capital expenditures of the government. Those receipts of the government which create liability or reduce financial assets may be called capital receipts. Main components of such receipts are borrowing of different kinds and repayment of loans and advances by other parties. Those expenditures of the government which lead to creation of physical or financial assets or reduction in recurring financial liability fall under the category of capital expenditure. Such expenditures pertain to payments on acquisition of assets like land, buildings, machinery, equipment as also investments in shares and loans and advances given to state governments, public sector enterprises and other parties. See also Zero-base Budgeting (ZBB).

Budget Deficit

It is a situation signifying shortfall of current revenue of the government below its current expenditure.

Budget Incidence

It relates to the combined effects of an equal increase in tax and public expenditure on the distribution of income. It is also called net incidence and is obtained by summing, algebraically, both the tax incidence (negative) and expenditure incidence (positive) for each of the subgroups of the population.

Buffer Stock

It refers to the stock of a commodity (say wheat) kept to meet fluctuations in its demand and/or supply so as to keep its price under check. It is thus a residual between supply and demand. When demand is less than supply it stores the residual and when demand is greater than supply it supplies the residual.

Built-in-stabiliser See Automatic Stabiliser

Buoyancy and Elasticity of Tax Revenue

These terms refer to the degree of responsiveness of tax yield to changes in national income.

Tax revenue may change through automatic response of the tax yield to changes in national income and/or through the imposition of new taxes, revision of the bases and/or the rates of the existing taxes, tax amnesties, stricter tax compliance and other administrative measures backed by legal action. Changes in the tax yield resulting from modifying tax parameters (bases, rates etc.) are called discretionary changes. Variations in the tax yield flowing from the combined effects of automatic responses as well as discretionary changes constitute the buoyancy of a tax. It is computed by dividing percentage change in tax yield by percentage change in national income.

With tax parameters held constant (i.e. discretionary changes being removed), automatic changes in the tax yield resulting from variations in the national income measure the elasticity of a tax system. It is the ratio of percentage change in tax revenue (adjusted for discretionary changes) to percentage change in national income.

Buoyancy estimates assess the overall success of government measures to increase tax revenues while elasticity coefficients indicate the inherent responsiveness of a tax system to changes in national income. In the absence or weakness of elasticity attribute of the tax system, a government will have to revise tax rates and tax bases every year to keep the share of tax revenue in national income undiminished. Such frequent changes complicate tax laws, reduce administrative efficiency and are also politically inexpedient. Therefore, tax structure should be so designed as to impart reasonable degree of elasticity to it.

Business Cycles

Business cycles (also called trade cycles) are long-term patterns of fluctuations in economic activities in an economy. They are characteristic of a capitalistic economy.

Buy at Home Campaign

It refers to prejudice for buying things produced domestically. This tendency accentuated during the 1930s depression when *Buy British*, *Buy French* and *Buy American* campaigns were launched to expand domestic employment. In India, its local variant was *Swadeshi* movement.

Buyer's Market

It is a market situation in which supply is greater than demand so that buyers have a bargaining advantage. To reduce their excess stocks, sellers are forced to accept lower prices.

C

Call Money Market

This is the most important component of the organised money market located in metropolitan cities of a country. It deals in credit for very short period of time, less than 15 days, even 1 or 2 days. The main participants in this market are the commercial banks who are surplus/short of funds temporarily. It is also called *inter-bank call money market*.

C and F

It is an abbreviation for cost and freight. It is a price quotation that includes the cost of merchandise and freight charges for its shipment to a given destination. It does not include insurance of the shipment so that the buyer rather than the seller is responsible for any damage occurring during transit. See also C and I; and C.I.F.

C and I

It is an abbreviation for Cost and Insurance. See also C and F; C.I.F.

Canons of Taxation

These are principles or maxims used in the designing or evaluation of a tax or a tax system. Given the level of taxation in a country, fiscal experts can design a tax system which best promotes the objectives of economic policy with due regard to social justice.

Adam Smith (1723-1790), the famous 18th century British economist, was the first to set forth such maxims in his book *Wealth of Nations* published in 1776. The four general guidelines laid down by him for designing an ideal system of taxation are as follows:

1. Equity: According to Adam Smith, "The subjects of every state ought to contribute towards the support of the government, as nearly as possible, in proportion to their respective abilities, i.e. in proportion to the revenue which they respectively enjoy under the protection of the state."

Tax equity is the prime characteristic of a good tax system. It is the basic criterion for evaluating a tax system. This classical canon of taxation is based on the natural desire among people for justice.

An inequitable tax system hinders the establishment of a stable political, social and economic order. The French and American Revolutions were partly the result of perceived inequity in the tax systems. In India, the duty on salt which hit the poor the most symbolised national protest against the British rulers during the freedom struggle. Tax equity ensures better tax compliance because unjust tax systems induce people to evade taxes. If properly defined and effectively implemented, an equitable tax system can prevent concentration of economic power in a few hands.

Thus, equity consideration is of overriding importance for any tax system and for any particular tax. Equity level determines how the tax burden is distributed among the taxpayers.

Though highly desirable, the concept of tax equity is nebulous and value-laden, defying measurement. It is identified with such general notions as fairness, justice, and impartiality which in turn again defy quantitative measurement. There are two approaches to tax equity in the literature: 1. Benefit Principle of Taxation (q.v.) and 2.

Ability-to-Pay Principle of Taxation (q.v.). It is noteworthy that these two principles which are understood distinctly by modern economists were badly mixed up by Adam Smith in his above quoted passage.

2. Certainty: This Smithian dictum relates to the time, manner and the amount of tax payment. Adam Smith observed, "the tax which each individual is bound to pay ought to be certain, and not arbitrary." Uncertainty may subject taxpayers to the arbitrary decisions of the authorities, demoralise the honest taxpayers and breed social evils like bribery. Certainty about tax liability helps a taxpayer to effect necessary co-ordination between his income and expenditure with a view to discharge his tax obligation with planning. The canon of certainty requires that tax laws are well-defined and do not contain provisions which the government cannot, or will not, enforce effectively. Frequent changes in tax laws should also be avoided.

3. Convenience: The canon of convenience relates to the procedure adopted for collecting taxes. According to Adam Smith, "Every tax ought to be levied at the time, or in the manner, it is most likely to be convenient for the contributor to pay it." For instance, land revenue should be collected at the time of harvest and in the village itself. Similarly, provisions should exist in tax laws for postponement or remittance of the levy in case of poor harvest. Following the principle of convenience, many municipalities allow payment of property tax in instalments. Deduction of income tax at source and payment of taxes through banks are other examples of convenient compliance for the benefit of taxpayers. Deduction at source increases the speed of cash flows into public treasury and also reduces the possibility of tax evasion. The principle of convenience is further promoted if tax laws are simple and comprehensible by ordinary taxpayers.

4. Economy: Every tax involves some revenue yield and a corresponding cost of collection. The main items comprising the latter are wages of the officials and costs of materials. Adam Smith noted, "every tax ought to be so contrived as both to take out and to keep out of the pockets of the people as little as possible over and above what it brings into the public treasury of the state." Cost of collection when expressed as a proportion of tax revenue is called Cost-Yield Ratio (q.v.). It is indicative of the overall efficiency of tax administration. Thus, the lower the cost of collection, the more productive is the tax and vice versa.

The foregoing requirements of a good tax system are desirable when examined individually. However, serious problems arise when a mix of these principles is evaluated. Quite often these desirable elements are in conflict with each other and pose serious difficulties in formulating tax policy. For example, simplicity in tax laws may leave too much unexplained, giving ample discretion to tax officials. The simplicity argument may also run counter to the principle of equity if tax laws fail to take account of the varying circumstances of taxpayers. Similarly, there is an inherent conflict between canons of economy and equity. Equity demands, *inter alia*, the right to appeal but the provision for appellate tribunals increases the cost of tax administration.

In view of the inconsistency among several goals, it is difficult to achieve all of them simultaneously. Therefore, society has to trade-off some goals for others. Which objective should be pursued at the expense of which other and to what degree is a question difficult to answer. The solution must be sought with reference to a country's currently accepted goals of social and economic policies and the government's concern for them. It is also possible that principles of taxation are overlooked not because of conflict between them, but because of overriding political considerations.

Capital

It refers to all those man-made machines and appliances which are used for further production of goods and services rather than being consumed for their own sake.

Capital Allowances

These are deductions from business income for depreciation of assets used in business. These are allowed because fixed assets (like plant and machinery) are gradually used up in the production process. If their wear and tear is not taken into account, the taxable income will be overstated. Annual capital allowances traditionally take the form of a fixed percentage of the cost of an asset.

Capital Budget **See Budget**

Capital Coefficient **See Capital-Output Ratio**

Capital Consumption **See Depreciation**

Capital Expenditure

In the context of taxation of income, the distinction between capital expenditure and Revenue Expenditure (q.v.) is important because only revenue expenditure is allowed to be deducted while computing income. Capital expenditure is deductible to the extent of depreciation allowance permitted.

Tax laws rarely define capital expenditure and revenue expenditure. Based on their natural meaning and judicial pronouncements, the two terms are understood in the following manner: 1. Capital expenditure is incurred in acquiring fixed assets while revenue expenditure is made in the normal course of business. 2. Capital expenditure produces benefits for several years while revenue expenditure is consumed within the same year. 3. Capital expenditure is of non-recurring nature while revenue expenditure is incurred again and again.

Capital Flight

It refers to erratic outflows of capital from one country to another in order to earn profit or avoid loss which may occur due to exchange rate variations. For example, fearing a fall in exchange rate, speculators may move foreign currency out of the country and bring it back after devaluation when it is worth more. A comprehensive exchange control regime can check capital flight. See also Hot Money.

Capital Formation

The excess of production over consumption in a year is called capital formation. It is also called accumulation.

The entire production of a year is not consumed. Production is normally higher than consumption. The surplus of production over consumption in a year is defined as capital formation. Capital formation consists broadly of the following: 1. Construction of new assets like buildings, roads and bridges. 2. Production of machinery and equipment. 3. Increase in the stocks of raw materials, semi-finished goods and finished goods in a year.

Capital Gains

These gains arise from the sale of assets other than those held in the ordinary conduct of business. For example, gains from the sale of a house by the house owner are capital gains while gains from appreciation in the value of houses held by a real estate dealer are ordinary gains of business.

The procedure to compute capital gains involves the following steps: 1. Ascertain the full value of consideration received or accruing as a result of the transfer of the asset. 2. Deduct from the full value of consideration (a) the cost of acquisition of the asset including cost of any improvements made to the asset, and (b) expenditure incurred in connection with the transfer of such asset (brokerage, legal expenses etc.). See also Capital Gains Tax; Capital Loss.

Capital Gains Tax

It is a tax on the increase in capital value of an asset. Treatment of capital gains is a controversial issue in determining the scope of income for tax purposes. What is the justification for taxing capital gains?

According to *net accretion principle* (attributed to Robert Haig and Henry Simons), income is defined as net accretion to economic power between two periods of time, or what accrues to an individual over a period of time as measured by the amount of his spending plus net accretion to his wealth. Stated comprehensively, this definition of income takes into account (a) cash income, e.g. wages, interest and dividends received, (b) imputed income such as imputed rent from owner-occupied houses and (c) accrued income like interest credited (instead of paid) and appreciation in the value of assets which continue to be held (capital gains).

Thus, in terms of *net accretion principle*, capital gains should be taxed as part of income. This is justified both on equity and efficiency considerations. From equity angle, inclusion of capital gains in the income tax base is required because they represent, like other sources of income, net accretions to spending power. The case for taxation of capital gains is further strengthened for they accrue unevenly among the people because wealth itself is unevenly distributed. On efficiency grounds, taxation of capital gains is required as it discourages investment in unproductive assets (like gold, paintings, antiques etc.) and speculative activities.

It is sometimes argued that capital gains are unexpected and unsought for and therefore should not form part of taxable income. Disagreeing, James Cutt in his book, *Taxation and Economic Development in India* (1969), observed, "Even acceptance of the fact that a proportion of capital gains represent windfall or unexpected elements in no way diminishes the increase in satisfaction or increase in spending power derived from their acquisition. It is also far from certain that a substantial proportion of capital gains represent unintended, fortuitous receipts. Capital gains differ only in degree from other forms of income and are often deliberately sought."

The opponents of capital gains tax contend that gains resulting from inflation are illusory in real terms and therefore do not represent real increase in a taxpayer's spending power. Tax on capital gains, which merely compensate for the rise in price level, is more in the nature of a tax on wealth than on increments in the value of wealth. Undoubtedly, an inflation-proof tax system is more certain and equitable in an inflationary economy but this is an ideal situation for all sources of income and not for capital gains alone. Pragmatically, the solution lies in revision of exemptions and concessions in the light of inflation. Moreover, it is not unreasonable to assume that real estate prices move upward more quickly than the general index of prices.

To compensate for the inflationary rise in the value of an asset, it is often suggested to increase the acquisition cost by the rate of inflation in the period between acquisition and realisation. However, taxation of capital gains only on realisation enables a taxpayer to postpone his tax liability until the date of realisation, conferring on him an interest earning advantage. According to J.E. Meade Committee Report on *The Structure and Reform of Direct Taxation* (1978), "The benefit of deferral is a loan free of interest of an amount equal to the tax liability on accrued gains. Thus, suppose that a gain of £100 accrues in 1975 and is realised in 1977. With a rate of tax of 30 per cent, £30 in tax is paid on a realisation basis in 1977 instead of in 1975. The taxpayer has kept the £30 for two years free of interest. If the tax paid in 1977 is to reflect this fact, then the £30 should be grossed up at compound interest for two years. To achieve this result, it would be necessary to mark up the deferred tax liability by an interest rate factor. This process can be contrasted with the allowance for inflation, where it is necessary to mark up the acquisition cost by an inflation factor."

The Meade Committee devised a formula for reducing tax burden according to inflation factor and increasing it by interest factor. Apparently, the net effect would depend upon the rate of inflation and the interest rate assumed.

Critics argue that taxation of capital gains discourages transfer of assets (e.g. selling and buying of shares or real estate) and therefore restricts the mobility of capital. Since transfers occasion a tax, investments remain tied up in their present form. The argument is weak because most transfers are speculative in nature and are not related to issues in economic development. It is the investment in new equity, rather than the existing one, which ensures a higher rate of growth. In short, there exists a case for taxing capital gains.

Realised Versus Unrealised Capital Gains: Normally, the scope of capital gains tax is restricted to realised capital gains. Even in the case of realised capital gains, a selective approach is followed because it is neither desirable nor practicable to tax capital appreciation of all types of assets. It would be unwise to ask a taxpayer to report capital gains arising from the sale of his washing machine or some other household article. In practice, the scope of capital gains tax is restricted to realised capital gains from the sale of stocks, real estate, jewellery etc. Even these assets pose serious problems because valuation is required both when an asset is bought and when it is sold. Valuation is simple for shares quoted in the stock exchange but it is difficult in case of assets which are not regularly traded in the market. There is no escape from the valuation problem and the tax administration has to grapple with it.

Taxation of unrealised capital gains is more controversial. Various arguments against and for taxation of unrealised capital gains are best summarised by R.A. Musgrave and P.B. Musgrave in their famous book *Public Finance in Theory and Practice.*

Against: Unrealised gains should not be taxed because the owner has refrained from consumption.

For: Absence of consumption is not relevant in defining the base of an income tax.

Against: Unrealised gains should not be taxed because in the absence of realisation we do not know whether they really exist.

For: Measurement of unrealised gains may be difficult, but this is not an insuperable obstacle.

Against: Taxation of unrealised gains requires the owner to pay a tax even though he or she has not obtained cash with which to pay it

For: As would be necessary with other debts that may become due, it is not unreasonable to ask the taxpayer to liquidate a part of his or her assets to make the tax payment if needed.

Against: For income to be received, it must be separated from the asset.

For: Separation is a matter of investment choice whereas income accrues when the asset value is increased.

Strictly speaking, unrealised capital gains are part of accretion (to wealth) and should be included in the definition of income for tax purposes. In the long-run, the distinction between unrealised and realised capital gains is not important because unrealised gain is realised at one time or the other during the life time of an individual or at the time of his death. Because the sums of unrealised and realised gains equal, the life-time tax obligation of an individual is said to remain the same provided there are no significant changes in the rate structure. Despite the foregoing theoretical justification for taxing unrealised capital gains, it is difficult to incorporate them in tax laws in view of various practical problems. For one, it would require valuation of capital assets each year, imposing considerable burden on administration. It is relatively easy to estimate accrued capital gains each year for some assets (like regularly quoted ordinary shares) but for most other assets it would be a Herculean task. Therefore, tax laws invariably exempt unrealised gains and bring within the purview of taxation only realised capital gains.

Short-term Versus Long-term Capital Gains: Incidence of tax on capital gains depends upon whether such gains arise from the sale of a short-term or a long-term capital asset. Gains from the sale of assets held for less than a specified period are short-term while gains from the sale of assets held over that period are treated as long-term. Generally, short-term gains are taxable like ordinary income while long-term gains enjoy tax concessions.

Is preferential treatment of long-term capital gains justified? One argument in favour of such preferential treatment is that capital gains are irregular and therefore tend to suffer under a system of progressive tax schedule. In other words, preferential treatment is a compensation for the absence of income averaging provisions in tax laws. Against this disadvantage, there are certain advantages available to income in the form of capital gains. As already noted, there is an interest earning advantage for deferred tax payment on capital gains. Moreover, tax liability can be postponed indefinitely by not realising capital gains. If the gains are allowed to accumulate in this manner, they will ultimately be transferred in the form of gifts or bequests to other persons. To deal with such eventualities, gift and estate taxes provide the second line of defence. However, gift and estate taxes are neither regular nor effective components of tax structures in most countries. These taxes, which apply to value rather than change in the value of property, carry a wide amplitude of exemptions/concessions and therefore form a small proportion of total tax revenue even in most developed countries of the world. In some countries, these taxes do not exist and in others they have been abolished after unsuccessful experiments.

As a proxy for income averaging provisions, it is common in tax laws of countries to allow set off and carry forward of capital losses. In view of these safeguards, the concessionary tax treatment of capital gains is unjustified. Such preferential treatment provides a strong incentive, particularly at high bracket rate, to receive income in the form of capital gains rather than, say business profits. Such a tendency is not conducive to positive entrepreneurship in an economy.

Capitalism

It is a form of economic organisation characterised by private ownership of the means of production. A capitalist society like the USA exhibits the following features: 1. Right to private property prevails. 2. Law of inheritance operates. 3. Means of production are owned by private individuals or groups of individuals (companies and partnership firms). 4. These means of production are used for maximising profits for their owners. 5. Right of free enterprise is guaranteed. 6. There is competition among firms. 7. Price mechanism allocates resources.

Advantages: The chief advantages of capitalism are: efficiency in production, competition, hard work, risk taking, research and development and innovations. Initiative and efficiency are inherent in the capitalistic form of economic organisation.

Disadvantages: Recurrent business depressions are a great defect of capitalism. During a depression, the automatic controls of the price system fail, the industrial production is below installed capacity and there is widespread unemployment. Another disadvantage of capitalism is the presence of extreme economic inequalities. Capitalism also suffers from excessive emphasis on materialism, consumerism, selfishness and cut-throat competition.

Capital Levy

It is a one-time tax on existing wealth. It is different from annual tax on wealth. Such a drastic fiscal measure is resorted to during or after a war or some other national emergency. The purpose of capital levy is to reduce the size of national debt and relieve the inflationary pressure associated with it.

Through capital levy, a government may appropriate not only an individual's income from capital, but also a part of the capital itself. Many of the individuals may not be able to pay capital levy from their liquid assets and hence be forced to sell a portion of their securities and real estate.

Administration of a capital levy is by no means an easy task. Fair valuation of capital held by millions of persons in a country is extremely difficult, particularly when financial and real estate markets are underdeveloped. Inexact valuation and tax evasion are likely which may cause serious inequities and disorganisation.

If payment of capital levy is compulsory in the form of money, many taxpayers will be forced to liquidate their assets, causing depression and disruption in the capital and real estate markets. In case any kind of asset is acceptable as payment, the government faces the gigantic task of disposing of a large variety of assets.

In Britain, capital levy was often advocated in post-war periods as a means of taxing wealth acquired during war. It was used only once in that country in 1948 in the form of once-for-all special contribution. Austria, Hungary, Germany, and Czechoslovakia imposed capital levy during the First World War, and Italy during the inter-war period.

Capital Loss

It is a decrease in the value of an asset. In terms of the net accretion principle, capital losses are set off against capital gains and net capital losses are treated as a reduction in income (economic power) of an individual. See also Capital Gains; Depreciation

Capital-Output Ratio

It is the ratio between the book value of plant and machinery and gross value of output of a firm. Also called *capital coefficient,* it measures capacity utilisation and capital intensity of a firm/industry. See also Incremental Capital-Output Ratio.

Capital Receipts

Those receipts of an organisation which create liability or reduce assets are called capital receipts. Thus, money obtained by way of loan, from the sale of fixed assets, issue of shares and debentures are capital receipts. They are generally of a non-recurring nature.

Capital receipts are exempt from income tax unless they are expressly taxable whereas Revenue Receipts (q.v.) are taxable unless they are expressly exempt from tax.

Capital Transfers See Current and Capital Transfers

Caribbean Community and Common Market (Caricom)

Founded in 1973 with headquarters at Guyana. it consists of Jamaica, Trinidad and Tobago, Guyana, Barbados, Belize, St. Lucia, Grenada, St. Vincent and the Grenadines, Dominica, Antigua and Barbuda, St. Kitts and Nevis, Bahamas Anguilla and Montserrat.

Carry Back of Losses See Loss Carry Back

Carry Forward of Losses See Loss Carry Forward

Cartel

A cartel is a combination of firms constituted with the objective of restricting competition in the market so as to maximise profits. Formation of cartels is illegal in most countries of the world. However, secret collusions are quite common.

In the context of international trade, when two or more producers/producing countries having major control over the production of some commodity, join to form an association or group with a view to control its output, distribution and price, a cartel is considered to have emerged with its behaviour similar to that of a monopolist. It can be formed at national or international level. A well-known example of cartel in recent years is the Organisation of Petroleum Exporting Countries (OPEC). See also Anti-trust Policy.

Cascading Effect

This concept is associated with a traditional turnover tax which is levied on transaction of goods and services at all levels of production and distribution. For example, Excise Duty (q.v.) may be levied on raw materials, components, semi-finished and finished goods. This system of taxation increases the price of a commodity much more than the tax collected, resulting in *cascading*. The price of a finished product reflects the taxes imposed on inputs used.

If middlemen apply fixed percentage mark-up to purchase price as their profit and if the purchase price includes taxes, the mark-up will be applicable to the tax component of the purchase price as well. Thus, increase in the price of a commodity will be more than the tax element.

Cash Basis Accounting

Under cash basis accounting, as against Accrual Basis Accounting (q.v.), a record is kept of actual receipts (cash incomings) and actual payments (cash outgoings) of a particular year. Thus, income collected during the Previous Year (q.v.) is taxable whether it relates to the previous year or a year preceding or following the previous year. Similarly, expenditure actually incurred during the previous year is deductible irrespective of the fact whether it relates to the previous year or some other year.

Similarly, tax revenues of a government may be recorded either on cash basis (the time at which the tax payment was received by a government) or on an accrual basis (the time when payment became due without incurring any penalty). Under cash basis reporting, taxes due in one year but actually paid in the following year and taxes withheld by the employer in one year but paid to the government in the following year, are both included in the receipts of the following year. Cash basis reporting is preferred because it shows the amount of tax revenue actually available to a government.

Casual Income

Refers to income which is non-recurring in nature. It is produced by chance, accident or fortune. It is neither calculated nor settled nor is there any likelihood of its coming at a certain time. In some countries, casual income up to a certain level is exempt from income tax. For example, under Section 10(3) of the Indian Income Tax Act, 1961, casual income is exempt from tax up to Rs. 5,000.

Central American Common Market (CACM)

It was established in 1960 with headquarters in Guatemala and with the intention of encouraging economic integration among its members, namely Costa Rica, Guatemala, El Salvador, Hondurus and Nicaragua.

Central Bank

Central bank of a country is usually a government owned and operated institution that controls the banking system and money supply in the economy. It is responsible for (a) issuing currency, (b) managing money supply, (c) administering rate of interest, (d) monitoring borrowing and lending policies of commercial banks, (e) undertaking governmental banking activities and (f) maintaining foreign exchange reserves, external value of money and a country's balance of payments.

Central banks of the leading Western nations (Federal Reserve in the United States, Deutsche Bundesbank in West Germany, Bank of Japan, and Bank of England) generally work closely to improve the global monetary system and to conduct varying degrees of co-ordinated currency support actions in times of severe exchange or other financial problems.

Central bank of a country uses various instruments to control and regulate the supply of money and credit in the economy.

Open Market Operations: The central bank can enter the money market for the purpose of purchase or sale of government securities on its own account. Every open market purchase by the central bank increases primary money by equal amount while every sale decreases it. As regards their advantages, open market operations are highly flexible, easily reversible in time, their effect on money supply is immediate, and they do not carry *announcement effects* as in the case of changes in the bank rate. Open market operations, considered very effective in developed countries, are not of much importance in LDCs due to underdeveloped nature of money and capital markets

Variable Cash Reserve Ratio: In most countries, commercial banks are required statutorily to hold cash reserves with the central bank. Apart from required reserves, the banks also hold excess reserves of cash. A large proportion of these excess reserves are held in the form of cash in hand or vault cash to meet the withdrawal needs of the depositors and the remaining part with the central bank to meet the net loss of cash due to the cross-clearing of cheques among the banks.

Bank Rate Policy: As lender of the last resort, the central bank helps the commercial banks in temporary need of cash when other sources of raising cash are exhausted. An increase in the bank rate would discourage commercial banks to borrow from the central bank and a corresponding increase in the lending rate of commercial banks to general public would decrease public borrowings from the banks.

Moral Suasions: Through moral suasions, the central bank can influence the investment and credit policies of the commercial banks. For example, it can ask the commercial banks to invest a larger proportion, than required, of their assets in government securities. Similarly, it can advise them regarding the allocation of credit to the private sector.

Centrally Planned Economy **See Command Economy**

Cess

A levy, usually on plantation crops (tobacco, jute), to raise funds for research and improvement schemes related to those crops (e.g. high-yielding variety of seeds). A cess is different from a tax in that the proceeds of the former are used for the benefit of industry on which it is levied.

Ceteris paribus

Most economic laws hold good under several assumptions. Although techniques have been developed (multiple regression) to study the influence of several independent variables on a dependent variable simultaneously yet it is desirable, for the sake of simplicity, to ignore the influence of relatively unimportant factors on the dependent variable. Therefore, it is usual to make the ceteris paribus (other things being equal) assumption under which all but one independent variables are held constant so as to study the influence of the independent variable (not held constant) on the dependent variable.

Change in Stock

At the beginning of a year, every enterprise possesses some stock of raw materials, half-finished goods and finished goods which could not be sold in the previous year. This is called opening stock. At the end of the year, it is left with some stock of intermediate goods or raw materials, semi-finished goods and finished goods. This is called closing stock. The difference between the opening stock and closing stock is the change in stocks.

Change in stock = closing stock – opening stock

Charitable Purpose

In many countries, income of charitable trusts is exempt from tax subject to certain conditions. Generally, a trust should be one established in accordance with law and its objects should fall within the definition of the term charitable purpose. Section 2(15) of the Indian Income Tax Act, 1961, defines charitable purpose to include relief of the poor, education, medical relief, and the advancement of any other object of general public utility not involving the carrying on of any activity for profit.

Cheap Money

It is a situation in which credit is easily available at relatively low rate of interest.

C.I.F.

Abbreviation for cost, insurance and freight. It is a price quotation that includes cost of merchandise, shipping insurance and freight charges to a specific destination. It is generally applied to imports to work out their prices. It includes F.O.B. (q.v.) value of a commodity plus the cost on insurance and transportation to the importing country.

Classical Economics

The very best of all financial plans is to spend little. This famous dictum of Jean Baptiste Say (1767-1832) aptly summarises the views of classical economists who dominated European economic thinking during the 18th and 19th centuries. Their leader Adam Smith (1723-1790) restricted government's duties to the following activities in his epoch-making book *The Wealth of Nations* (1776).

1. The duty of protecting the society from violence and invasion by other independent societies; this, of course, is the function of national defence.

2. The duty of protecting every member of society from injustice or oppression of every other member of society. This reflects the obligation of establishing an administration of justice which provides law and order within the society so that market economy may function.

3. The duty of establishing and maintaining highly beneficial public institutions and public works which are of such nature that the profits they could earn would never repay the expense to any individual or small number of individuals to provide them.

4. The duty of meeting the expenses necessary for support of the sovereign, which vary depending on the form of political structure.

Other activities, such as government enterprise, were declared unjustifiable by Adam Smith and his followers. Excessive public expenditure leads to excessive taxation and the latter was considered an obstacle to a country's march towards industrialisation.

The classical ideas had always been based on the hypothesis that an economic system, via price mechanism, normally tends to equilibrium, i.e. full employment of all the productive forces. Any deviation from the equilibrium was attributed to incidental and temporary friction, which could ultimately be eliminated by the automatic working of price mechanism. Classical economists postulated full employment because they believed that unlimited wants create unlimited possibilities of production. There was no room for permanent instability in their system. They also assumed that the productivity of government services was nil. In short, they believed that the best government is that which does the least.

Classical economists were principally preoccupied with the relationship between business firms and between the various economic classes participating in production: landowners, investors, wage earners and business enterprises. This micro level approach had led them into an examination of prices, land rent, interest, wages and profits. The classical economists paid no attention to the solution of the problems of business depressions and unemployment. They believed that the influences of demand and supply would bring about such an adjustment of individual relationships that the economy would tend to a high level of activity and full employment of its own accord. Occurrence of depressions and unemployment would be temporary in character and self-correcting. They firmly believed in Say's Law (q.v.) that there is always enough demand for all the goods that can be produced, they reasoned that there must be enough demand for all the labour and all the capital that are available to produce them. The economic process will tend toward a condition of full employment. There could be unemployment of labour or capital at local levels of the economy because of lack of adjustment between specific demands and specific supplies. The possibility of prolonged general unemployment was ruled out.

This theory of employment propounded by classical economists was based on the assumption that receipts of money income by factor suppliers are approximately equal to their spending on consumption or investment goods. This assumption, they believed was close enough to the facts of real life. However, the occurrence of serious business depressions from time to time seemed to belie them.

The ideas of the classical school were respected and followed by the European statesmen up to the first half of the 19th century. However, as the Western economies grew complex in the wake of the Industrial Revolution, it became increasingly difficult to maintain the rigidities of Smithian prescriptions. The rapid industrialisation was accompanied by its own problems like unemployment, exploitation of labour, economic fluctuations, and balance of payments difficulties. Governments could no longer afford to remain silent spectators. Faith in economic automatism was shaken and that in intervention started growing. European governments started drifting away from classical ideals in the latter half of the 19th century. The First World War aggravated the urgency of state interference, and the depression of the 1930s proved to be the last straw on the camel's back. The entire philosophy of the classical economists crumbled like a house of cards.

From the chaos of the depression grew the ideas of John Maynard Keynes (1883-1946) which hold good (at least for the developed world) till date. Keynesian economics rejects the normality of full employment hypothesis. On the contrary, it believes that there is generally a discrepancy between the demand for and the supply of goods, and to restore the balance between the two a general programme of action is required. During times of depression, production, national income, and employment are at a low level. The functioning of price mechanism is imperfect and consequently the ill-effects of depression cannot be successfully tackled at the micro level. The most efficient way to obtain or to maintain full employment is the governmental financial policy. Through public work programmes, employment can be raised to a higher level thereby increasing the demand for goods and services. All this can be achieved through the medium of budget. Hence, the importance of budgetary policy and government intervention.

Indeed, the classical concept of passive public finance has given way to functional finance to deal with the complexities of modern economies which require constant monitoring on the part of fiscal authorities to avoid various disequilibria. Furthermore, there is increasing realisation that left to itself the market mechanism cannot perform all economic functions optimally. The premise that market mechanism leads to efficient use of resources, i.e. it produces in the cheapest way what consumers want the most, is based on the following assumptions: 1. There is perfect competition in the factor market as well as in the commodity market. 2. Individuals can be excluded from consuming goods if they do not pay for them. These conditions are rarely fulfilled in practice. Monopolistic and oligopolistic tendencies replace competitive forces to rob capitalism of its virtues.

State intervention becomes necessary to curb such tendencies to protect consumers' interests. Even if it is assumed that competition is assured in the factor and commodity markets, still certain goods, because of their peculiar production and consumption characteristics, cannot be provided through market mechanism. In view of the problem of externalities, certain services (like defence, and street lighting) have to be provided through the public sector.

Classification of Taxes

There are several ways of classifying taxes. The Organisation for Economic Co-operation and Development (OECD) has classified taxes in a straightforward and business-like manner. Though this classification ignores economic nature of different taxes, it has proved very useful for inter-country tax comparisons. OECD classification groups different taxes into categories and sub-categories like taxes on goods and services, taxes on income, profits, and capital gains, taxes on net wealth and immovable property, taxes and stamp duties on gifts, inheritances etc. OECD classification of taxes is as follows:

OECD Classification of Taxes

1000 Taxes on income, profits and capital gains

1100 Taxes on income, profits and capital gains of individuals

1200 Corporate taxes on income, profits and capital gains

2000 Social security contributions
2100 Employees
2200 Employers
2300 Self-employed or non-employed

3000 Taxes on payroll and workforce

4000 Taxes on property
4100 Recurrent taxes on immovable property
4200 Recurrent taxes on net wealth
4300 Estate, inheritance and gift taxes
4400 Taxes on financial and capital transactions

5000 Taxes on goods and services
5100 Taxes on production and sale of goods and rendering of services
5200 Taxes on use of goods

6000 Other taxes
6100 Paid solely by business
6200 Paid by other than business

Clean Float

It refers to floating exchange rate not involving central bank's intervention to support the exchange rate. See also Dirty Float.

Closed Economy and Open Economy

A country which has no economic relations with other countries of the world is a closed economy. All other countries except the one under consideration are grouped into one category called the rest of the world.

A country which has economic relations with the rest of the world is an open economy. These economic relations consist of the following: 1. Selling goods and services to foreigners (exports). 2. Buying goods and services from the foreigners (imports). 3. Buying shares, bonds, debentures from foreigners (acquiring foreign assets). 4. Selling shares, bonds debentures etc. to foreigners (incurring foreign liabilities). 5. Lending to foreigners and borrowing from foreigners. 6. Sending gifts to foreigners and receiving gifts from them. 7. Residents of a country going abroad to work there and foreign residents coming and working in the domestic territory of the country.

Cobb-Douglas Production Function

Named after its authors, Paul H. Douglas and Charles Cobb, it is a linear and homogeneous production function yielding constant returns to a proportionate increase in the use of all inputs. It takes this form, $Y = kL^{a}C^{(1-a)}$ where Y represents income (output), L is the quantity of labour input, C is the capital employed and k and a are positive constants (and $a < 1$).

Cobweb Theory **See Stable and Unstable Equilibrium**

Coefficient of Determination **See Correlation**

Collateral

It is an asset which serves as security for a loan.

Collective Bargaining

It refers to negotiations between a trade union (representing workers) and the employer for the purpose of determining/improving conditions of employment including wage rate, hours of work, retirement benefits etc.

Command Economy

Resource allocation and income distribution can be accomplished by means of the command principle. In this case, the individual economic units are ordered as to how productive resources are to be allocated among competing uses and what technique of production is to be adopted. These commands are derived from some sort of conscious attempt (planning) to co-ordinate the activities of the individual units and to direct the economy as a whole towards certain definite goals. The command principle implies: (a) little independence on the part of the individual economic unit, (b) presence of superior authority that issues the commands, (c) hierarchical organisational structure and (d) co-ordinating planning on which the commands are based.

A socialist society does not possess a self-adjusting market mechanism. Instead, the adjustment has to be a conscious decision of planners who receive information on disturbances. At times the response to a disturbance may take the form of the creation of new institutions or the substantial reform of old institutions. Through trial and error procedures, the system adapts itself to the changed conditions. Centralisation has its own advantages. The first is to safeguard public interest and priorities. Yet another reason for centralising decisions relates to what the economists call external economies.

Commercial Bank

A commercial bank is a financial intermediary which accepts deposits of money from the public and lends them with a view to make profits. A post office may accept deposits but it cannot be called a bank because it does not perform the other essential function of a bank, i.e. lending money. Similarly, some other institutions like Unit Trust of India may be lending to others but since they do not accept chequable deposits, they cannot be termed as banks. They are non-banking financial institutions.

A commercial bank generally performs the following functions:

1. It accepts deposits which are of various types like current, savings, recurring and fixed deposits.
2. It grants credit in various forms such as loans and advances, discounting of bills and investment in open market securities.
3. It collects cheques, drafts, bills and other instruments for its depositors.
4. It provides remittance facilities through drafts and telegraphic transfers.
5. It renders investment services such as underwriter and banker for new issues of securities to the public.
6. It provides such agency services as purchase and sale of foreign exchange, acceptance of tax payments, electricity bills etc.
7. It provides facilities like travellers cheques, gift cheques and safe deposit vaults to its customers.

Through mobilisation of resources and their better allocation, commercial banks play an important role in the development process of underdeveloped countries. By offering attractive saving schemes and ensuring safety of deposits, commercial banks encourage willingness to save among the people. By reaching out to people in rural areas, they help convert idle savings into effective ones. Commercial banks improve the allocation of resources by lending money to priority sectors of the economy. These banks provide a meeting ground for the savers and the investors.

Commercial Bill

It is a marketable instrument and an important device for providing short-term credit to business and industry. Commercial bills (or bills of exchange) are issued by business firms. Business firms often sell goods on credit and the buyers promise to pay the value of goods after a specified period of time, say 3 months. Thus, a bill with a maturity period of 3 months is like a post-dated cheque to be honoured by the buyer of goods. The holder of the bill may need cash before the maturity date and in that case he can sell it to some other person or to a bank at a discount.

Bills are of two types: (a) demand bills which are payable on demand or presentation or sight as, for example, a bank draft and (b) time bills which are payable after a stipulated time period, generally 3 months.

Commercial Invoice

It is a basic export document containing all the information which is required for preparing *all other* documents. It gives the description of the exporters and importers, their names and addresses, goods and their prices, terms and conditions and name of the shipping vessel. The description of the goods should tally fully with that given in the Letter of Credit (q.v.).

Commercial Policy

It refers to a country's official policy towards foreign trade, tariffs, quotas and non-tariff barriers. It also deals with the composition and direction of a country's foreign trade.

Commodity Agreements

These are agreements among producer countries of primary products (sugar, copper, coffee, cocoa, tin) to control prices and export volumes in the world market. Under such agreements, export quota of each member country is fixed. However, problems arise in the implementation of such agreements when signatory countries do not stick to their quota or do not agree on the quota allotted to them.

Commodity Tranche **See International Monetary Fund**

Common Market

It is a form of regional grouping in which member countries agree to (a) abolish all tariff restrictions on the movement of goods within the market, (b) have common external tariff for non-member countries and (c) permit free movement of factors of production from one member country to another.

Commonwealth Preference

Formerly Imperial Preference, the term is used to refer to the policy of granting a preferential tariff to countries of the British Empire.

Under Commonwealth Preference, certain imports into Britain are charged import duty at reduced rates or are admitted free of duty, provided that the products have been grown entirely in a Commonwealth country.

In principle, the preferential system is contrary to the Most Favoured Nation (q.v.) clause accepted by the erstwhile GATT under which no special privileges in trade should be established between countries without these privileges being made available to all. See also Preferential Duty, and Discriminating Duty.

Company Taxation **See Corporate Income Tax**

Comparative Advantage, Theory of

It is also known as theory of comparative cost. Propounded by British classical economist David Ricardo (1772-1823) to explain the basis for international trade, it states that trade takes place between two countries due to differences in the cost of production between them. One country may be more efficient than another in the production of every commodity (efficiency measured by factor inputs per unit of output); but it may be more efficient in the production of some commodities than others. According to Ricardo, a country should specialise in and export those commodities in which its comparative cost is less, i.e. comparative advantage is more. Alternatively, a country having disadvantage in the production of all commodities should specialise in and export that one in which its comparative disadvantage is less.

Suppose two countries A and B both produce machinery and textiles with the same production function employing only one factor of production, say labour. Country A uses 10 units of labour to produce a given machine and 6 units of labour to produce a given length of textile. Country B produces the same unit of machinery and textile with the help of 15 units and 7 units of labour respectively. Clearly, country B is producing both the goods at higher labour cost. It means country A is having absolute advantage in the production of both. Observing closely, we find that country A's comparative advantage is more in machinery where the cost ratio is 10:15 or 2:3 than in textiles where the ratio is 6:7 or 2:2.3

According to this theory, country A should specialise in and export machinery where its comparative advantage is more while country B should specialise in and export textiles where its comparative disadvantage is less. Specialisation of this kind will bring both of them a bigger market and economies of scale leading to further reduction in the cost of production. Hence, both the countries will gain from trade.

Comparative Cost, Theory of See **Comparative Advantage, Theory of**

Compensation of Employees

It is defined as payments made by employers in the form of wages and salaries to their employees, in cash and in kind. It also includes contributions made by employers in respect of their employees to social security schemes, private pension, family allowance, casualty allowance, life insurance and such other schemes.

Compensatory Duty

It is a tariff levied on the import of a commodity to match some other tax which a country has imposed on local production of the same commodity. It is levied so that domestic producers are not put to any disadvantage.

Compensatory Finance

Economic role of the government is very important in modern societies. A government should conduct its activities in such a way as to provide stability to the economy at high level of employment and national income. The instruments used for compensatory finance are taxes, subsidies, borrowings and spending. If business activities begin to decline, the government should reduce taxes, thereby leaving more money in the hands of the public. This would encourage them to spend more, helping the revival of the economy. At the same time, the government should embark on public works projects that involve expenditure and the employment of labour. The expenditure should be financed by printing of money so that more money is put into circulation to boost business activities.

Competitive and Complementary Economies

Two economies are said to be competitive if due to similar factor endowments and tastes, they are producing a similar range of goods. Conversely, complementary economies are less overlapping in the nature and type of goods they produce. Whether member economies are competitive or complementary affects the success of a Customs Union (q.v.).

Compliance Costs of a Tax

Compliance costs refer to costs incurred by taxpayers or third parties in complying with a tax, over and above the tax payment made to public authorities. The third party compliance costs are those incurred by firms in discharging their legal responsibility as tax collectors, e.g. deducting income tax from salaries and passing it on to the tax authorities.

Three types of compliance costs may be distinguished: (a) Money costs like payment for legal advice, fees to accountants or to valuers for valuation of property (for purposes of death duties, wealth tax etc.), cost of postage, telephone calls, travelling, books, and in some cases litigation. (b) Time costs include time taken to consult tax advisers, complete tax returns, and to travel to tax offices. (c) Psychic costs are the worries and anxieties associated with tax payment.

Administrative costs plus compliance costs make up the total operating costs of a tax.

Compound Duty

Duties of excise and customs are generally levied on *ad valorem* or specific basis. Sometimes, both specific and *ad valorem* duties are levied on a single item. This is called specific-cum-*ad valorem* duty or compound duty. See also *Ad Valorem* Duty, and Specific Duty.

Compounded Levy

Levying of excise duty on the production of small-scale sector is a major problem of tax administration. The procedures adopted for collection of excise from large-scale units are often found expensive and time-consuming when applied to small firms. Under compounded levy, a lump sum payment is made on the basis of some installations, e.g. the number of looms in a textile unit. Once the compounded levy is paid, the producer becomes free from all excise formalities except to maintain a record of looms in operation.

Conference on International Economic Co-operation and Development (CIECD)

It is an organisation formed in September 1975 in Paris in which 8 industrial countries (of the North) and 19 developing countries (of the South) including OPEC were made the members. It was meant to deal with (a) heavy debt burden contracted by some of the more advanced developing countries due to high oil import prices (b) the ways to sustain their growth rates and (c) the slow down of growth in the OECD countries and the ways to check it.

Conglomerate

It refers to production units selling unrelated products which are united into one big business firm.

Consignment Tax

It is a levy on inter-state transfer of goods. A consignment is a despatch or a stock-transfer from a company to its branch located in a different state. Since no sale is involved, it is called in-house transaction by a company. Sometimes, unscrupulous parties evade payment of inter-state sales tax by showing virtual sales as consignments from one state to another. By this method, the payment of inter-state sales tax is avoided. This problem was faced by the tax authorities in India. Hence, through a Constitutional amendment the Central Government was empowered to levy taxes on the consignment of goods (whether the consignment is to the person making it or to any other person), where such consignment takes place in the course of inter-state trade or commerce.

However, trade circles maintain that consignments become necessary in view of seasonal fluctuations in the demand for goods as well as frequent transport bottlenecks. Commercial practices like branch transfer or transfer on consignment basis also help manufacturer-supplier to reduce avoidable costs of holding high level of inventory.

Conspicuous Consumption

It refers to consumption intended to display one's money power. The concept, introduced by Thorstein Veblen (1857-1929) underlines general tendency among almost all sections of society to outshine their neighbours/relatives by purchasing superior goods even though these are beyond their means. Conspicuous consumption has adverse effects in a developing country because it reduces savings for investment purpose.

Constant Returns to Scale **See Returns to Scale**

Consumer Sovereignty

Under capitalism, consumer is said to be sovereign in the sense that ultimately those commodities are produced which are demanded by the consumers. In other words, consumer preferences determine, through price mechanism, the level and pattern of production.

However, many doubt the so-called sovereignty of the consumers in a free market economy. It is perhaps the sovereignty of the class which has the purchasing power. Moreover, under monopoly capitalism, consumer preferences are manipulated by the big corporations through advertising. The market mechanism reflects the preference pattern of giant corporations rather than the needs of the people.

Consumer Surplus

This concept in economic theory was introduced by British economist Alfred Marshall (1842-1924). It refers to the difference between the price that a consumer *actually* pays for a commodity and the price that he would be *willing* to pay for it. Consumer surplus is a measure of the satisfaction that a consumer gets from a commodity, over and above the sacrifice (as measured by its price) that he makes to acquire it.

Consumption

Consumption is the destruction of utility. Using up of goods and services to satisfy human wants is defined as consumption. There is no time gap between the production and consumption of services. Goods, particularly durable goods, may continue to provide services for quite some time. However, like services, all goods are treated as consumed the moment they are purchased. The only exception is the purchase of houses by the households. Houses are treated as capital goods. Consumption is counted at the point when the commodities are purchased for consumption. Material goods destroyed in accidents, fires, floods, earthquakes, wars, riots are excluded from consumption because they do not serve any purpose.

Consumption Function

British economist John Maynard Keynes (1883-1946) formulated the relationship between consumption and the level of disposable income (consumption function). He believed that the change in consumption is less than the change in disposable income. Though Keynes believed that consumption is principally a function of disposable income, he did recognise the influence of non-income factors on the level of aggregate consumption. He classified non-income determinants of consumption into subjective and objective factors. Subjective factors reflect psychological preferences, e.g. buying attitudes which in turn are influenced by advertising, attractiveness of the product, expectations about the price level and future availability of goods. Objective factors include distribution of income, cost and availability of consumer credit and stock of assets.

Economists have analysed consumption data with a view to establish empirically the influence of income and non-income factors on consumption.

Absolute Income Hypothesis: It maintains that an individual consumer's spending depends on the absolute level of his income. When this theory is extended to aggregate behaviour, it indicates that increase in the aggregate income of all consumers leads to a decline in the Average Propensity to Consume (q.v.). As the level of aggregate income grows larger and larger, the APC becomes smaller and smaller. However, statistical records show that consumption function is proportional in the long-run. How this difference is sought to be reconciled? It is reconciled by stating the effects of the following non-income factors.

1. With the increase in the accumulated wealth of households they tend to spend a larger fraction of income. This shifts the consumption function upward.

2. The continuous movement of population from rural areas to urban areas also contributes to upward shift in consumption function. Urban wage earners have a substantially higher propensity to consume.

3. The percentage of older people in the population increases over the long-run period. Per capita consumption in this age group does not drop off as rapidly as does per capita income.

4. New consumer goods are introduced over the long-run period.

According to the absolute income hypothesis, factors like these cause the consumption function to shift upward thereby producing a proportional relationship between consumption and income. If income factor alone is taken into account, one would expect non-proportional relationship.

Relative Income Hypothesis: The relative income hypothesis was developed by American economist James Duesenberry. According to him, consumption and saving decisions are greatly influenced by social environment in which one lives. Thus, an individual with a given income consumes more if he lives in an affluent neighbourhood than if he lives in a poorer one.

When this hypothesis is extended from individual consumer behaviour to aggregate behaviour, the ratio of consumption to income becomes dependent on the ratio of the current income level to the peak income level previously attained. In developing the peak income argument, Duesenberry relies on the known fact that income does not grow at an even pace over the long-run but instead displays cyclical ups and downs. These short-run income fluctuations push the economy off the long-run curve and onto the successive short-run curves in an unbroken series over time.

If the income falls due to recession, consumers will cut down their savings more than proportionately in an attempt to maintain the previously established higher standard of living.

The aggregate behaviour suggested by the relative income theory may be expressed in a single consumption function that combines the properties of the long-run function (C = bY) and the short-run function (C = Ca + cY) as follows:

$$C = Y (b - c) + cY$$

Permanent Income Hypothesis: American economist Milton Friedman believes that consumption is not based on the current level of disposable income. According to him, current disposable income Ym is composed of permanent income Yp and transitory income Yt. Permanent income is that which households expect to receive over an extended number of years, while transitory income consists of any unexpected addition to or subtraction from permanent income. Thus, Ym = Yp + Yt.

The theory holds that permanent income determines consumption. In addition, it assumes that households, regardless of their level of permanent income, consume approximately the same proportion of their permanent income. In other words, the basic relationship between aggregate consumption and aggregate income is proportional but the relationship is expressed in terms of permanent income and consumption.

In the permanent income hypothesis, the basic point is the effect on consumption of the positive and negative transitory income components that appear as income departs from the long-run growth path during business cycles.

Life Cycle Hypothesis: According to this hypothesis, an individual family seeks to maintain a stable or gradually increasing level of consumption over its life cycle. Its income displays a distinctly different pattern over the same period of years. The APC varies significantly from a maximum at the early and late years to a minimum at the peak earning years of the life cycle.

What happens to the aggregate consumption of all families as their aggregate income varies over time? The answer depends, among other things, on what happens to the distribution of families by age and by income over time. If there is an increase in the proportion of all families who are at the early and late stages of the life cycle, it may result in a rise in the fraction of the larger total income that is consumed. The opposite shift in the age distribution would appear to have the opposite effect.

Consumption of Fixed Capital **See Depreciation**

Continuous Variable **See Variable**

Corn Laws

They refer to 19th century tariff restrictions put by UK government on its grain imports from European Continent. These were advocated by landed aristocracy which wanted to retain high agricultural prices but were strongly opposed by the newly emerging industrial class (also by David Ricardo) because these meant rise in wages of industrial labour. Corn laws were repealed in 1846.

Corporate Income Tax

It is levied on the earnings of corporations. A corporation (or a company) is regarded as a separate entity for purposes of income tax. Total income of a corporation is arrived at with reference to its profits shown in its profit and loss account. To such profits (or losses) are added those expenses which, though actually incurred by a corporation, are disallowed, partially or wholly, under the law. From this total, the amount of tax concessions is deducted to arrive at the taxable income of a corporation. Rate structure of corporation tax may be progressive or proportional depending upon the tax policy of a country.

Issues in Corporate Income Tax: Various questions arise regarding the tax treatment of corporation profits.

1. Should corporations be taxed at all on their profits? A tax on the profits of corporations is a common feature of industrial societies. Absence of corporation tax would encourage business firms to form corporate entities to avoid personal income tax by retention of profits.

2. Should corporation tax discriminate between retained and distributed profits? Under one scheme known as split rate method, distributed profits may be taxed at a lower rate than retained profits. However, such a distinction causes complexity in tax laws. Therefore, corporation profits are generally taxed without making a distinction between retained and distributed profits.

3. There is a view that corporation profits should be distributed among the shareholders and then taxed at the shareholders' level (under the individual income tax) instead of at the corporation level. The taxes due to shareholders on dividends may be withheld at the corporation level to be credited subsequently under the individual income tax. In

practice, most countries tax corporation income separately resulting in Double Taxation (q.v.) of corporate earnings. Tax laws often contain provisions to mitigate this kind of tax duplication.

Interaction Between Corporate and Individual Income Tax: Corporation tax is related with individual income tax in, at least, three ways.

1. Under the classical system (as prevalent in the United States), a corporation is viewed as a separate entity distinct from its shareholders and therefore taxed in its own capacity. The liability of a corporation is divorced entirely from that of the shareholders so that dividends are taxed twice, first as income of the corporation, and subsequently as income of the shareholders.

2. Under the full integration system (or full dividend imputation system), a corporation is not seen as a separate entity from its shareholders. The corporation tax is treated as a withholding tax which is credited in full to shareholders. This credit is used against personal income tax, which is due on their imputed share of corporation profits.

Under the partial imputation system, a shareholder is given credit against some part of his own personal tax liability. Australia introduced a system from July 1, 1987 under which Franked Dividends (q.v.) paid out of income already subject to corporation tax carry a credit to individual shareholders. Originally, the system represented a full integration of the corporation and personal tax regimes because corporation tax rate and maximum personal tax rate were same (47 per cent) and therefore no personal tax was ever payable on franked dividends. However, following a reduction in the rate of corporation tax to 39 per cent, a taxpayer subject to the top personal rate of 47 per cent is now subject to additional tax on dividends. Hence, the integration is partial instead of full as was the case initially.

3. Then, there is the split rate system which lies between the above two extremes. Under it, relief is provided through a lower tax rate on corporate distributions than on retained profits.

Corporation Tax **See Corporate Income Tax**

Correlation

Economic analysis has often to deal with problems involving the use of two or more than two variables. If two quantities vary in such a way that movements in one are accompanied by movements in the other, these quantities are said to be correlated. The statistical tool with the help of which the closeness of relationship between variables is measured is called correlation. The measure of correlation, which summarises in one figure the direction and degree of correlation, is called *correlation coefficient*.

In business, correlation analysis enables the policymakers to estimate costs, sales and prices on the basis of some other series with which these may be functionally related.

Positive Correlation: If both the variables vary in the same direction, as one is increasing the other is also increasing or if one is decreasing the other is also decreasing, correlation is said to be positive.

Negative Correlation: If the variables vary in opposite directions, i.e. as one variable increases the other decreases or vice versa, correlation is said to be negative.

Simple Correlation: When only two variables are studied it is a case of simple correlation.

Partial Correlation: In partial correlation, more than two variables are recognised, but only two variables are considered to be influencing each other, the effect of other influencing variables being kept constant.

Multiple Correlation: In multiple correlation, three or more variables are studied simultaneously, e.g. the study of the relationship between the yield of paddy per acre and the amount of rainfall and the amount of fertilisers used.

Linear Correlation: If the amount of change in one variable tends to bear a constant ratio to the amount of change in the other variable then the correlation is said to be linear. If such variables are plotted on a graph paper, all the plotted points will fall on a straight line.

Non-linear (Curvilinear) Correlation: Correlation will be called non-linear or curvilinear if the amount of change in one variable does not bear a constant ratio to the amount of change in the other variable. In most of the practical cases, a non-linear relationship between the variables is observed.

Of the several mathematical methods of measuring correlation, Karl Pearson's method, popularly known as Pearsonian coefficient of correlation, is most widely used in practice. The Pearsonian coefficient of correlation is denoted by the symbol r. The value of r lies between -1 and +1.

Coefficient of Determination: A convenient and useful way of interpreting the value of coefficient of correlation between two variables is to use the square of coefficient of correlation, which is called coefficient of determination. The coefficient of determination is denoted as r^2. If the value of r = 0.9 then r^2 will be 0.81 and this would mean that 81 per cent of the variation in the dependant variable is explained by the independent variable. The r^2 is also defined as the ratio of the explained variance to total variance.

r^2 = Explained variance (0.81) / Total variance (1)

The ratio of unexplained (0.19) variance to total variance is called the coefficient of non-determination and is denoted by K^2 and its square root is called the coefficient of alienation (as against correlation) denoted by K.

Correlation and Association: Characteristics possessed by individual items of a data are either numerical or descriptive. Characteristics which are capable of quantitative measurement (weight, height, age) are numerical while those which cannot be quantitatively measured (nationality, religion, sex) are descriptive. Observations based on numerical characteristics are called statistics of variables while observations based on descriptive characteristics are termed as statistics of attributes. The relationship between variables is the subject-matter of correlation theory; the relationship between attributes is discussed by the theory of association. See also Regression.

Cost-Benefit Analysis See Social Cost-Benefit Analysis

Cost of Production

Profit maximisation is the objective of all firms. Profit is the difference between revenue and cost. It is, therefore, necessary to know how cost and revenue vary with output. The study of cost behaviour of a firm is more important because a producer can influence his cost by varying the proportions of factors of production, or by economising on the use of factors, or through better and more efficient co-ordination of factors. Under perfect competition, the price of the product is determined by market forces and a firm has to sell at that price. In other words, a firm has no control over its revenue (price) and it can earn more profit only by reducing its cost of production. Any firm that is trying to maximise its profits must also try to produce a given output at lowest possible cost.

The term cost has various meanings in economics.

Real Cost and Money Cost: Production process involves exertion on the part of labour, abstinence on the part of saver, and risk-taking on the part of entrepreneur. In other words, production process involves pain, discomfort and disutility for factors of production. These exertions of labour and abstinences of savers constitute, according to British economist Alfred Marshall (1842-1924), the real cost of production. Obviously, the notion of real cost is subjective and defies measurement and hence has little practical utility.

In the real world, it is the money cost of production which is more important for the producer and the economist. Money cost refers to monetary payments by a firm to different factors of production which help the firm to produce a commodity. Thus, wages paid to labour and payment made for capital borrowed, raw material, equipment, transportation etc. all form part of money costs of a firm.

Explicit Cost and Implicit Cost: A producer hires factors of production for use in the production process. Apart from the hired factors, he also uses factors owned by him. He makes payments to factors which do not belong to him. Such payments relate to wages of labour hired, interest on borrowed funds, rent of hired lands and buildings etc. These are all explicit costs of production. However, the producer does not make payments for the factors which belong to him and are used in the production process. Thus, he has not to pay (a) any rent for the buildings owned by him, (b) any interest for his own funds invested in the business or (c) any salary to himself for his own services rendered in running the business. Yet, one cannot ignore the services of a firm's own factors in calculating the cost of production. This is so because a firm could have earned a return by supplying its factors to other parties. Thus, a firm which uses its own resources incurs implicit costs equal to the amount it could have earned by offering these resources to other users. In other words, implicit costs are the costs of using a firm's own factors of production. Both explicit and implicit costs are taken into account while studying the cost structure of a firm.

Opportunity Cost: It is well known that resources of an economy are limited and can be put to alternative uses. A hectare of land may be used to produce say 100 quintals of wheat or 75 quintals of rice but it cannot produce both the items simultaneously. If a farmer decides to cultivate the hectare of land for wheat production, he will have to forego the amount of rice which he could have produced instead of wheat. Thus, 75 quintals of rice is the opportunity cost of producing 100 quintals of wheat. Hence, opportunity cost (also called user cost) denotes the output sacrificed or foregone when a society uses resources for one product rather than another. It is called so because one forgoes the opportunity of producing a commodity when another commodity is produced instead.

Private Cost and Social Cost: Private cost is simply the money cost of producing a commodity by a private producer. It includes all explicit and implicit costs of production. The concept of social cost is broader. Apart from private cost, the production process may generate socially undesirable effects like pollution of air and water by private factories. Pollution, in turn, may adversely affect health of the people. Thus, social cost consist of private costs plus other costs (pollution etc.) imposed on society at large.

Fixed Cost and Variable Cost: Total cost is divided into two parts: total fixed cost (TFC) and total variable cost (TVC). In the short-run, some factors (machinery, equipment etc.) are fixed in quantity. Total fixed costs are those which are incurred by a firm for all fixed inputs. Apparently, these costs do not vary with output, i.e. they remain the same whether output is more or less or even zero. Total variable costs are those which are incurred by a firm for all variable inputs (labour etc.). These costs vary positively with output, i.e. they rise as more is produced and fall as less is produced. Fixed costs are also called *overhead costs* or *unavoidable costs*. Likewise, variable costs are also called *direct costs* or *avoidable costs*. Thus, TC = TFC + TVC.

Total Cost (TC): Total cost is self-explanatory. It is simply the total cost of producing a given level of output.

Average Cost (AC): Average cost or per unit cost is the total cost of producing a given level of output divided by the number of units produced. As in the case of total cost, average cost (AC) is divided into average fixed cost (AFC) and average variable cost (AVC). AFC equals total fixed cost divided by output while AVC equals total variable cost divided by output. Thus,

$$AC = \frac{TC}{X} = \frac{TFC + TVC}{X} = AFC + AVC$$

Marginal Cost (MC): Marginal cost is the increase in total cost resulting from increasing the output by one unit. Marginal cost of producing the 10th unit (or the nth unit) of a commodity is the change in total cost when production increases from 9 units (n-1 units) to 10 units (n units). Symbolically, $MC = TC_n - TC_{n-1}$.

A hypothetical numerical example showing relationship between output and various type of costs is given in the Table below.

Total, Average and Marginal Costs at Various Production Levels (Rs.)

Units of output	TFC	TVC	TC	AFC	AVC	AC	MC
1	60	30	90	60	30	90	-
2	60	40	100	30	20	50	10
3	60	45	105	20	15	35	5
4	60	56	116	15	14	29	11
5	60	75	135	12	15	27	19
6	60	120	180	10	20	30	45
7	60	185	245	8.5	26.4	35	65
8	60	276	336	7.5	34.5	42	91

Cost-push Inflation

It is a situation of price rise caused by decrease in supply due to enhanced cost of production. Cost of production may increase due to higher wages, higher taxes and difficulty in procuring basic inputs. See also inflation.

Cost Sharing Agreements

These are agreements on the basis of which different member countries contribute to international bodies like World Bank, International Monetary Fund, and United Nations to help them run their operations. Bases of contribution include national income, per capita income and a country's capacity to provide foreign exchange.

Cost-Yield Ratio

It is the cost of collection expressed as a proportion of tax revenue. A lower cost-yield ratio is considered indicative of the efficiency of tax administration. Unusually high cost-yield ratio is a drag on public exchequer. Thus, cost-yield ratios may be used to evaluate administration of competing taxes.

The concept of cost-yield ratio suffers from various limitations and therefore needs to be used carefully as an index of tax efficiency. The ratio depends upon the nature of a tax. Generally, cost of collecting direct taxes is high as compared to indirect taxes. The ratio is also affected by the nature of tax administration. If separate administration is used for each tax, the scope for scale economies is greatly reduced. Conversely, if a single administration deals with a variety of taxes of similar nature (e.g. all direct taxes), cost-yield ratio may fall due to scale economies.

Cost-yield ratio is also influenced by the nature of an economy. The ratio is generally high in developing countries which are in the process of evolving their tax systems. Widespread illiteracy and lack of accounting practices make assessment procedures extremely difficult in these countries.

Pointing out another limitation, G.K. Shaw has observed, "The cost-yield ratio provides a purely static insight into the efficiency of a given tax which may be misleading in terms of the potential dynamic evolution of the tax. Thus, for example, a tax in its infancy may have high costs associated with the establishment of the appropriate administration and collection machinery and yet its future prognosis may be favourable if it is progressively based or confronts income elastic demand conditions."

It is noteworthy that reduction in cost of collection which leads to ineffective enforcement and hence tax evasion, is false economy. Similarly, employment of incompetent and/or inadequate staff can result in harassment of taxpayers and multiplying appeals and hence increased cost of compliance. Properly understood, the principle of economy requires lowest possible costs consistent with effective administration and existing level of facilities to taxpayers. While interpreting cost-yield ratio, account should also be taken of compliance costs which may differ from tax to tax.

Countervailing Duty

It is a duty in addition to the normal import duty levied on goods imported into a country. The rate of countervailing duty is generally equal to the excise duty imposed on like items produced domestically. The argument is that normal import duty represents the desirable degree of protection to internally produced goods which are not subject to excise duty. When excise duty is levied or the rate of an existing one is increased, a corresponding enhancement in import duty is required to preserve the accepted degree of protection.

Cournot's Equilibrium **See Doupoly**

Crawling Peg

An idea developed by J. H. Williamson whereby a country facing a fundamental disequilibrium in its balance of payments and aiming at a change in exchange parity, should make its intentions public and change the exchange rate very gradually and slowly, say a maximum of 1 per cent a week. This will make speculation unattractive. This would influence payment flows by slowly bringing about price adjustments. The idea of crawling peg is in contrast to Adjustable Peg (q.v.) of the Bretton Woods system under which changes in par values are sudden, infrequent and in a sizeable, discrète step.

Credit

By credit we mean finance made available by a lender to a borrower. The personal resources of an entrepreneur are generally inadequate to undertake production on large-scale. He needs credit to start production and use modern technology. There are various classifications of credit, each with its own significance.

Sources of Credit: Credit may be classified on the basis of who provides it ? Sources of credit can be divided into two categories: (a) institutional sources and (b) non-institutional sources. Institutional sources are further sub-divided into: (i) banking sources (commercial banks) and (ii) non-banking sources (e.g. Unit Trust of India). Non-institutional sources include moneylenders, relatives, friends and other private parties.

End-uses of Credit: Credit may be classified on the basis of the use to which it is put. The two main categories of end-uses are: (a) production and (b) consumption. The production category is further sub-divided into: (i) industry, (ii) agriculture and (iii) trade.

Period of Credit: Credit may be classified term-wise into the following categories: (a) short-term credit, i.e. credit for a period of 1 year or less, (b) medium-term credit, i.e. credit for more than a year but less than 5 years and (c) long-term credit, i.e. credit for a period of more than 5 years.

Credit Policy See Monetary Policy

Credit Tranche See International Monetary Fund

Cropping Pattern

Cropping pattern refers to the distribution of cultivated land among different crops grown in a country. Cropping pattern reveals the nature of agricultural operations as, for example, the importance of food crops vis-à-vis cash crops.

Cropping pattern is influenced by a host of factors which can be classified into two broad categories: (a) physical factors and (b) economic factors. Among the physical factors, the following are important: soil conditions, extent of rainfall and type of climate. Economic factors include relative prices of agricultural commodities, size of the farms, availability of inputs, demand conditions, system of land holding and government policy regarding exports/imports, taxes and subsidies.

Cross Elasticity of Demand

If there are two commodities x and y, then cross elasticity of demand is the ratio of percentage change in the demand for commodity x to percentage change in the price of commodity y.

$$E_{xy} = \frac{\text{Percentage change in the demand for x}}{\text{Percentage change in the price of y}}$$

If x and y are substitutes, cross elasticity is positive. Contrarily, if x and y are complements, the cross elasticity is negative.

Cross Rates

Suppose the exchange rate between US dollar and German mark is $1 = 3 DM in New York, and the dollar-franc rate is $1 = 6 francs in Paris, then in Bonn the mark should sell for 1 DM = 2 francs. This derivation of exchange rate is known as cross rate. This is an example of orderly cross rate.

However, there will be a disorderly cross rate if in Bonn the mark sells for 1 DM = 3 francs rather than for 2 francs. It is disorderly because the appropriate exchange rate between the franc and the mark as determined by the two exchange rates with the dollar is 2 francs.

Cross-section Analysis

It refers to analysis of economic data for different countries at the same period of time. It is contrasted with time series analysis which measures changing situation in a country at successive points in time.

Crowding-out

The term is descriptive of any group/section being pushed out of a market. In the context of financial market, the demand for credit by the government and other public sector institutions may be so strong and inflexible that credit requirements of households and companies are crowded-out.

Cum Bonus and Ex Bonus

Cum bonus means *with bonus,* i.e. a quotation of a share where the right to bonus is transferred to the buyer. Ex bonus means *without the attached right to the bonus just announced,* i.e. the market quotation of a share where such a right is retained by the seller.

Cum Dividend and Ex Dividend

Cum dividend means *with dividend*, i.e. market quotation of a share where the right to receive the dividend immediately due is transferred to the buyer. Ex dividend means *without the attached right to the dividend just due*, i.e. a market quotation of a share where such a right to dividend is retained by the seller.

Cum Interest and Ex Interest

Cum interest means *with interest,* i.e. market quotation of an interest bearing security where the right to receive the interest payment immediately due is transferred to the buyer. Ex interest means *without the attached right to interest just due,* i.e. the market quotation of a debenture where such interest on it is retained by the seller.

Cum Rights and Ex Rights

Cum rights means *with rights*, i.e. market quotation of a share where the benefit of rights issue offered by the company is transferred to the buyer. Ex rights means *without the attached rights to new shares issued by the company*, i.e. market quotation of a share where such rights are retained by the seller.

Currency

Hard Currency: It refers to currency with full and easy convertibility and its conversion taking place at a nearly stable exchange rate and without any control of the country's monetary authorities to which that currency belongs. The assumption here is that the country concerned has a large foreign exchange reserve and a surplus in balance of payments.

Soft Currency: It is a currency with limited convertibility.

Inside and Outside Currencies: Currencies of member countries of an economic grouping (like European Union) are known as inside currencies while those of non-members are called outside currencies. For example, French franc and Italian lira are inside currencies in European Union while US dollar is an outside currency.

Exotic Currency: It refers to currency not having a developed international market and which is infrequently dealt with.

Currency Area

It refers to a group of countries having close economic and political ties and whose exchange rates are keyed to each other and are usually defined in terms of one currency of the group. They float as a group with respect to the rest of the world. This arrangement is a compromise between fixed and floating rates.

Currency Band

This refers to the maximum permitted range of fluctuations of a given currency against a reference currency.

Currency Clause

It is a clause is an export contract which specifies that the foreign currency (say pound sterling) payable for the goods shall vary in line with the market exchange rate of the local currency (say rupee) so as to maintain a constant (rupee) value of exports.

Currency Convertibility

External Convertibility:. It is a situation where convertibility is enjoyed solely by non-residents.

Internal Convertibility: Under it, conversion of a currency is permitted only for the residents of the country.

Partial Convertibility: If conversion of a currency is applicable only in terms of certain other currencies or only for certain transactions (mostly on current account of balance of payments) or only for a few institutions or persons, it is considered to have only partial convertibility.

Current and Capital Transfers

Transfers made from the current income of the payer and added to the current income of the recipient for consumption expenditure are called current transfers.

Capital transfers are defined as transfers in cash and in kind made out of the wealth/savings of the donor for the purpose of capital formation by the recipient.

Current Asset **See Asset**

Customs Co-operation Council Nomenclature (CCCN)

Customs Co-operation Council is a global organisation meant to cover all areas of customs techniques including customs classification, valuation and enforcement. CCCN (originally Brussels Tariff Nomenclature) is the internationally recognised standard classification of goods in world trade for customs purposes. It provides a common customs language to simplify international tariff negotiations.

Customs Co-operation Council was renamed as World Customs Organisation on January 26, 1995.

Customs Duty

It is a tax on the import and export of goods levied by a national government and payable to it when the goods cross the customs boundaries of the nation. Hence, it is also called border tax.

The term customs duty as an English expression originated in England during a period of disagreement between the King and the Parliament over the King's right to collect it. King's supporters claimed that the sovereign had been vested with the authority to impose this levy by a long established custom. Hence, it is suggested that from this the term customs duty was derived. The right was claimed on the ground that customs duties were a reasonable return to the King for the protection and security he was supposed to provide on land and sea.

Customs duties are probably the most ancient form of taxation. They are as old as international trade itself. Just as domestic production flows provide the base for excise taxation, so also international trade flows are the basis for customs duties. These duties are levied either on *ad valorem* basis (i.e. as a percentage of the value of goods imported or exported) or on specific basis (i.e. as a stated amount per unit of weight, volume etc.). Customs duties can be classified into two categories: import duties and export duties.

Import Duty: It is levied on the domestic value of the imported goods calculated at the official exchange rate. There are two main objectives of import duty: (a) to raise revenue for the government (revenue tariff) and (b) to discourage imports in order to protect a nation's domestic industry (protective tariff) or to correct a disequilibrium (deficit) in its balance of payments. Other measures to protect indigenous industries from foreign competition are import licensing, import quotas and outright import ban.

Export Duty: It is levied on export values expressed in domestic currency. Export duties can become an important source of revenue when a country enjoys comparatively strong position in respect of certain goods in the international market. Thus, when there is considerable disparity between the domestic and international prices of certain goods, levy of export duties is justified to mop up a part of the profits of exporters. Export duty on an item is levied after considering such factors as domestic production, likely exportable surpluses, demand for the item in the foreign markets, changes in exchange rates and prices prevailing in the international market.

Customs Union

It is established between two or more countries if all barriers (like tariffs and quotas) to trade amongst them are removed and, at the same time, a common tariff is adopted against non-members. This assures a free movement of all products within the union. In 1922, Belgium and Luxembourg formed a customs union and after World War

II it was enlarged to include the Netherlands and came to be known as Benelux.

A customs union is different from a free trade area in which each member country retains its own tariffs vis-a-vis non-members.

When member countries of a custom union remove all tariff barriers amongst themselves, more trade is supposed to take place. Each member country gets its goods from the cheapest source in the union. It adds to the welfare of all the member countries. This is referred as *trade creation effect*. On the other hand, since the union continues to apply tariff restrictions on non-member countries, their goods continue to be taxed and therefore they become costly relative to the goods produced inside the union. As a result, member countries divert their imports from non-member countries to member countries which are producing the same product. This movement or inter-country substitution is known as *trade diversion*.

Advantages of a customs union get reflected in the growing economies of scale due to expansion in size of market and production. More internal and external economies, greater effectiveness of competition and higher levels of investment and employment are some of the ways in which economic integration exhibits its advantages. As a result, all member countries experience a faster rate of economic growth.

D

Dead-weight Loss

It is a condition that benefits no one. See also Excess Burden of Taxation.

Dead-weight Tonnage (DWT)

It is the number of tons (each ton = 2240 pounds) of stores, fuel and cargo which a ship can transport. In countries where metric system is prevalent it refers to tonnes.

Dear Money

It refers to the policy of monetary restraint followed by the central bank of a country. By raising rate of interest and through other means, the central bank tries to reduce credit supply in order to relieve inflationary pressures in the economy.

Death Duty See Estate Duty

Death Rate

It is defined as the number of deaths per thousand of population in a country during a year. In demography, it is termed as crude death rate.

Debt Equity Ratio

It is calculated by dividing all debt by all equity capital of a company.

Debt to Net-worth Ratio

It is the ratio of the total liabilities of a company to its net worth.

Debt Trap

It is a situation in which a government is unable to repay its past loans without fresh borrowings

Declining-balance Depreciation Method

This depreciation method allows larger deductions in the early years of the useful life of an asset and smaller deductions towards the later years. The depreciation allowed is computed by multiplying a fixed rate by the asset's book value. Unlike the historical cost, the asset's book value declines from year to year by the amount of depreciation accumulated in earlier years. See also Straight Line Depreciation Method.

Decreasing Returns to Scale See Returns to Scale

Deductions

Deductions mean all amounts which are eligible for subtraction from gross receipts of a business. Strictly speaking, a deduction relates to an actual outlay e.g. expenditure on travelling. Tax laws must clearly specify as to which sums are allowed as deductions from gross receipts in order to determine the amount on which a given set of rates is to be applied.

Thus, a taxpayer is allowed, as a matter of practice, to deduct from his gross receipts the expenditures incurred to earn income. Since the net income basis of income tax is universally accepted, expenses related to producing or receiving income (i.e. income production costs) must be allowed as deductions from gross receipts. That the income tax should be based on a net income concept is necessary because if a gross concept is adopted, the tax would fall partly on expenditure (for earning income) instead of exclusively on income. It is the net income which represents ability-to-pay taxes.

Which expenditures are really incurred in connection with income production and to what extent they should be allowed as deductions from gross receipts are baffling questions for the tax designers. Familiar examples are the entertainment expenses of companies and the use of company cars. It is often difficult to identify such expenses and even if it is possible to do so, problems arise in deciding whether they were personal or related to business. Income tax laws generally elaborate allowable and disallowable deductions.

Deductions for Dependants

Basic exemption under an income tax law relates to an individual. However, individual income earners usually do not live alone but are heads of a family consisting of a spouse, children and sometimes dependant parents.

Basic exemption of the same order for bachelors and married couples with children is unfair. Family income remaining the same, the standard of living per capita of a couple with two children will be lower than that of a childless couple which in turn will enjoy a lower living level as compared to a bachelor. Relief based on the number of dependants is a levelling up mechanism between families of different sizes. Thus, it satisfies the principle of horizontal equity which requires similar tax treatment of people in similar economic circumstances.

Though conforming to the canon of equity, relief granted for children and dependants may clash with the population policy of a government. This is particularly the case in developing countries of Asia and Africa where population explosion has created serious socio-economic problems. The conflict between tax equity and demographic compulsions can be reduced if relief for the purpose is properly devised. Generally, an allowance of a fixed sum per dependant is allowed as deduction from taxable income. Alternatively, a tax credit per dependant is granted. Whichever system is followed, the relief must be given for a limited number of children and if that number is crossed, it should be curtailed or even withdrawn. For example, a 20 per cent credit against tax may be given for the first child and 10 per cent for the second child and if the third child is born, the overall credit be reduced by 10 per cent. In the event of the fourth child, the entire relief may just be withdrawn.

The principle of horizontal equity can further be promoted if account is taken of certain unavoidable expenses of abnormal nature. Two families of the same size and the same income will have different budget burdens if one family is all healthy while the other family has to look after a disabled child. A large number of special personal deductions (medical expenses, charitable contributions) exist in the income tax statutes of various countries.

Deductive and Inductive Reasoning

Economists use various methods to arrive at appropriate conclusions regarding observable economic phenomenon. Two of these methods are deductive and inductive logic.

Under deductive method, conclusions are deduced from certain generally accepted norms of human behaviour. In other words, the reasoning proceeds from the general to the particular. For example, it is an accepted truth that all producers try to maximise their profits. Hence, it is deduced that the firm under study also tries to maximise profits.

In the case of inductive method, the logic proceeds from the particular to the general. In other words, conclusions of individual observations are generalised. Thus, if the study of the behaviour of an individual consumer reveals that he tries to maximise his satisfaction, it can be induced that all consumers try to maximise their respective satisfactions.

Deficit Financing

Deficit financing is a kind of forced saving. When all types of government receipts fall short of its stipulated total expenditure, then the only alternative left with it is to print more currency. The net effect of deficit financing is to increase money supply in the economy. When money supply increases, it puts pressure on the supply of goods and services. Since supply cannot be increased so easily, prices have a tendency to rise. Price rise is accompanied by its own adverse effects because the burden of price rise falls inequitably on different classes. Deficit financing is a kind of inflation tax which drives the people into involuntary savings.

Magnitude, timing and consequences of deficit financing are controversial issues. In developing countries, governments are always on the lookout for more and more resources to finance development schemes. Taxes are by far the most important source of public revenue but a great part of this revenue goes to meet the administrative expenditure of governments. Next in importance are borrowings, internal as well as external. When this source is also exhausted, then a government resorts to deficit financing in order to claim a part of real resources of the economy.

Deficit financing is mainly resorted to during wartime or for development schemes. Apparently, if it is for the latter purpose, the ill-effects would be short-lived because as the development schemes mature, the improved production level will reduce inflationary pressure in the economy. Contrarily, if it is for war purpose, the adverse consequences are long-drawn, causing widespread dislocation in the economy.

In the initial stages of development, a modest dose of deficit financing may be justified on grounds of monetisation of the economy. When developmental activities pick up, the demand for money also increases because of increasing transactions. A controlled and gradual increase in money supply plays an important role by boosting investment in the economy.

However, a reckless monetary expansion may prove dangerous by aggravating inflationary tendencies. In a supply constrained economy, the Keynesian investment income multiplier operates more in money terms than in real terms. During inflation, fixed income groups are adversely affected and the poor suffer the most. Producers, distributors, speculators and hoarders are the gainers. In extreme cases, if inflation becomes uncontrolled, people may lose faith in the currency itself. Thus, no society can afford a continuous and significant rise in the general price level. It is rightly said that deficit financing like fire is a good servant but a bad master.

Deflation

It refers to decrease in the general price level in an economy.

Degree of Openness

Openness of an economy with respect to foreign trade refers to its permissiveness towards exports and imports. It is determined by the tariff and non-tariff restrictions it imposes on the flow of foreign trade. Openness is generally measured by the trade-GDP ratio of a country

Demand

It is common for us to see commodities being bought and sold in the market everyday. The buying and selling of a commodity takes place at a particular price. How are the prices of various commodities determined in the market? In a free enterprise economy, there are two forces which determine the prices: demand and supply.

In economics, demand means the quantity of a commodity which an individual is willing to purchase over a specific time period and at a specific price. Mere *desire* for a commodity is not demand. Mr. A may desire to have a motor car but if he does not possess the requisite purchasing power or he is not willing to spend it then his desire cannot be called demand. Thus, demand is the desire for a commodity backed by purchasing power and the readiness to spend it.

Demand for a commodity is determined by a number of factors. In other words, demand is a function of the price of the commodity, money income of the consumer, prices of the related commodities and tastes and habits. For example, the demand for sugar is a function of the price of sugar, income of the consumer, price of tea leaves (a related commodity) and taste. Symbolically,

$D_s = f(P_s, Y, P_t, T)$

Amongst all these factors, price of the commodity is the most significant one. Barring taste, all other determinants are quantifiable. The relationship between demand and its quantifiable determinants is now examined separately.

Theory of demand suggests inverse or negative relationship between the price of a commodity and the quantity demanded. At higher prices, the demand for a commodity is less and at lower prices it is more. Or, when the price of a commodity decreases, its demand increases and conversely when price increases, its demand decreases. This is called the *law of demand.* It is based on the assumption that other factors affecting demand for the commodity remain constant. This is the assumption of *ceteris paribus* (other things being equal).

For understanding the law of demand, we consider a hypothetical example of demand for sugar at various prices by individual A. We consider a demand function $Q_d = 7\text{-}P$. Based on it, the demand schedule of the individual is given in the Table below. The graphic representation of the demand schedule is called demand curve (see Figure below).

Demand Schedule of Individual A for Sugar

Price of sugar (Rs. per kg)	Weekly demand for sugar (kg.)
6	1
5	2
4	3
3	4
2	5

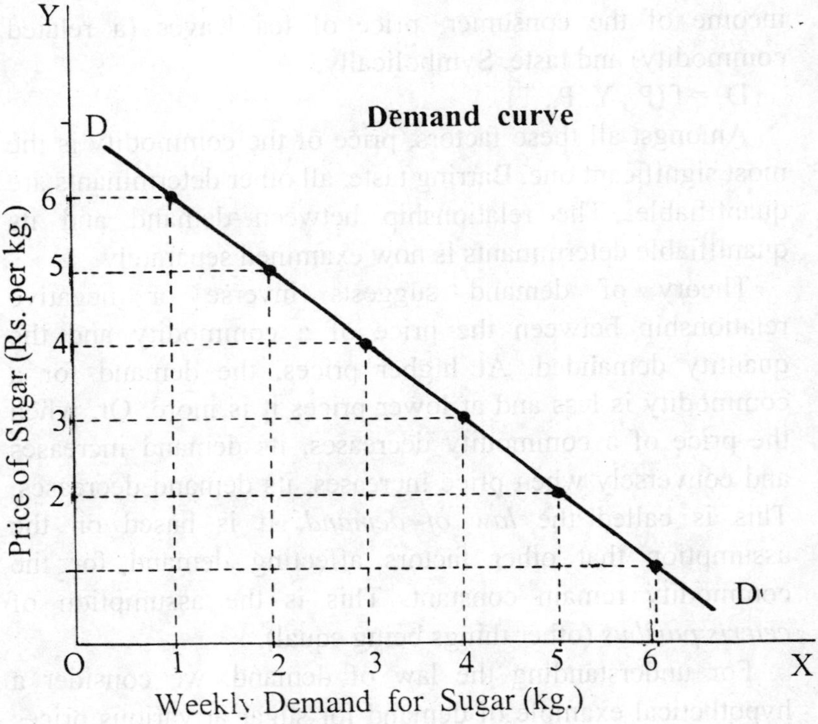

It is clear from the demand schedule as well as from the demand curve that individual A demands more sugar when price decreases and vice versa. The negative relationship between demand and price is shown by the downward sloping demand curve.

What are the reasons for the operation of the law of demand? Economists have given various explanations in this regard.

1. The law of demand is based on the law of diminishing marginal utility. The latter law, propounded by British economist Alfred Marshall (1842-1924), states that the consumption of the first unit of a commodity (say a cup of

tea) gives its consumer the maximum satisfaction. As he consumes more and more units of it, the successive units give him less and less utility. It means lower prices are needed to induce him to buy more and more units of the same commodity. In other words, when the price is lowered he would be willing to buy those units of the commodity which he did not consider worth buying before the fall in price.

2. A commodity may have different uses, some of which are more important than others. Thus, milk is used for preparing tea as also for making ice-cream. If the price of milk is very high, it would be used for the most essential purposes like feeding the babies and preparing the tea. When the price of milk declines, its use is extended to relatively non-essential purposes like preparing sweets. Hence, demand for milk increases.

3. Yet another explanation for the law of demand lies in what is called price effect. There are two components of the price effect: (a) substitution effect and (b) income effect.

Substitution Effect: Since consumers generally possess limited income, they have a tendency to substitute one commodity for another. A decrease in the price of tea relative to the price of coffee would encourage consumers to substitute tea for coffee. Substitution effect depends on individual preferences and the closeness of the substitutes available.

Income Effect: Money income of the consumer remaining the same, a decline in the price level means increase in his real income. Hence, he is better off, i.e. he has more purchasing power and can afford to buy more commodities. Because of positive relationship between income level and demand, a decline in price leads to increased demand.

Exceptions to the Law of Demand: The law of demand states negative relationship between price of a commodity and its demand. However, the law may not hold true under certain situations. Thus, the normal price-quantity relationship does not hold good in the case of special class inferior goods called Giffen goods named after British economist Robert Giffen (1837-1910) who pointed out this anomaly in the law of demand. As the price of a Giffen good decreases, the consumer becomes better off in real terms and therefore may switch over to the consumption of superior goods. A decrease in price leads to decrease in demand, violating the law of demand.

Another case pertains to the expectations of the consumers regarding future prices. Sometimes people wish to buy more of a commodity even when its price is rising. This is particularly the case during wars and other emergencies when people anticipate further increase in prices. Essential commodities like wheat and sugar are purchased not only to meet current consumption but also to provide for future consumption. Thus, increased demand in the face of increased prices leads to a situation running counter to the normal price-quantity relationship.

Likewise, the law of demand may not hold good for the behaviour of speculators. If the price of a particular share is declining in the stock market and the speculators expect a further fall in its price, the demand for that share will fall instead of rising.

It is true that in certain situations the law of demand does not operate but such situations are exceptions rather than the rule. For most commodities, the law of demand is a valid generalisation.

Relationship Between Demand and Income: Demand for a commodity is determined by a number of factors, including the income level of the consumers. Other things being equal, an increase in the income of a consumer generally leads to an increase in the demand for a commodity and vice versa. However, this is not always so. In fact, three types of relationship can be established between income and demand.

In the first case, there are commodities which are demanded almost in fixed quantity as, for example, salt, chillies and sugar. At very low level of income, a consumer may buy less sugar than required. As his income increases, his demand for sugar will also increase. However, after a certain level of income has been reached, his demand for sugar will stabilise. The second case pertains to inferior goods as, for example, maize. The demand for maize increases with increase in income up to a point but after that it starts falling when the income of the consumer exceeds a certain level. The third case relates to income-quantity relationship for normal goods like expenditure on entertainment, travelling, clothing and education. As income of the consumer increases, the demand for these commodities also increases. Most commodities fall under this category.

Relationship Between Demand for a Commodities and Prices of Related Commodities: The demand for a commodity may change even if we keep the price of that commodity and the income of the consumer unchanged. This becomes possible because the demand for a commodity is influenced by the prices of related commodities. Although the consumption of a commodity, in most cases, is related to the consumption of another commodity, this relationship is not always of the same nature.

In some cases, a commodity is useless in the absence of another commodity as, for example, motor car in the absence of petrol. Thus, goods are complementary (jointly demanded) when they are used together to satisfy a given want. In certain cases, the degree of complementarity is absolute as, for example, between tyre and tube. However, in other cases the degree of complementarity is weak as between shoes and socks. As a general rule, in the case of complementary goods a decrease in the price of one commodity (motor car) leads to increase in the demand for the other commodity (petrol) and vice versa.

Goods are substitute or competitive for one another if they satisfy the same want. Popular examples of such goods are tea and coffee, and various brands of soft drinks. As a general rule, in the case of substitute goods, a decrease in the price of one commodity (tea) leads to decrease in the demand for another commodity (coffee) and vice versa.

Demand-pull Inflation

It is a situation of price increase due to excess of demand over available supply. Excess of demand may be caused due to monetary expansion, panic buying and enhanced foreign demand. See also Inflation.

Demand Reversal

It is a situation in which a country having comparative advantage in a commodity has also such a large domestic demand for that commodity that internal production does not suffice. Hence, instead of exporting, which the theory of comparative cost would prescribe, the country is actually importing that commodity. This sets a strong limitation to the validity of the theory of comparative cost.

Demographic Transition, Theory of

According to this theory, propounded by A. J. Coale and E. M. Hoover, every country passes through the following three stages of demographic transition.

First Stage: During the first stage, the economy is rural and agriculture is the main occupation of the people. Techniques of production are primitive and per capita income is low. This type of economy is characterised by high birth rate and high death rate. High birth rate is attributable to widespread illiteracy, superstitions, absence of family planning methods and deep-rooted social and religious beliefs about family size. Likewise, death rate is also high on account of lack of medical facilities, poor sanitation and malnutrition. Thus, high birth rate is balanced by high death rate, and population remains stable or increases marginally. The first stage is marked by high growth potential of population but low actual growth.

Second Stage: It marks the beginning of the process of economic development. Living standard of the people starts improving. In this stage, death rate declines sharply owing to improved medical facilities, particularly eradication of mass-killing diseases like smallpox, cholera and plague. However, birth rate continues to remain at high levels because social and religious beliefs abcut marriage and family size take much longer time to change. Hence, high birth rate and falling death rate accelerate the growth of population. This stage is termed as the stage of *population explosion*. The high growth potential of the first stage is realised in the form of high actual growth of population.

Third Stage: In this stage, the economy moves from an agrarian to an industrial society. There is an increasing trend toward urbanisation and small families for achieving a higher standard of living. The economy is characterised by low birth rate and low death rate. Birth rate declines due to the spread of education and family planning methods. Otherwise also, a large family is a burden in urban industrial areas. Thus, the third stage is marked by low birth rate and low death rate, resulting in stable or marginally increasing population.

These three stages of demographic transition explain the transformation of a primitive high birth and high death rate economy into a low birth rate and low death rate economy.

Demonstration Effect

It refers to the desire among the people of underdeveloped countries to achieve higher standard of living of the developed countries. Through the modern means of communications (television, newspapers, tourism etc.) people in the underdeveloped countries have become aware of high living standards in the developed West. To follow suit they spend more and save less. As a result, imports increase and the country faces balance of trade deficit.

Density of Population

Density of population refers to the average number of persons living per square kilometre in a country.

Departmental Undertaking

A departmental enterprise, such as railways, is an unincorporated enterprise owned and operated directly by the Government. It is run on commercial lines and its working is assessed by financial performance, a criterion which distinguishes it from administrative activities of the Government.

A departmental undertaking is directly subordinate to a Ministry of the Government. It is financed by annual appropriations from the treasury and its revenues are paid into the treasury. It is subject to the budget accounting and audit controls applicable to Government activities. The employees of a departmental undertaking are civil servants and their conditions of recruitment and service are the same as for other civil servants. It can be sued only by following the procedure prescribed for filing suits against the Government.

The departmental form of organisation is considered more suitable in areas of strategic importance, requiring secrecy of operations. The ordnance factories, e.g. the Gun Carriage Factory, are under the charge of the Ministry of Defence. This form of organisation is preferred also for undertakings which provide services affecting the totality of the community or the security of the country. Thus, Indian Railways come under the charge of a full-fledged Ministry of Railways. Similarly, the operations connected with post and telegraphs are managed by a separate ministry.

The departmental system of organisation and management ensures effective Government control but suffers from the disadvantages of too much political interference, bureaucratic delays, and lack of initiative in decision-making.

Depreciation

Every producing enterprise possesses, at the beginning of the year, a certain amount of fixed capital in the form of buildings, machines and equipment. During the year, fixed capital goes down in value due to normal wear and tear which is not made good by current repairs and maintenance. Its value may also go down by foreseen obsolescence. Loss of value due to normal wear and tear and expected obsolescence is called *depreciation* or consumption of fixed capital or capital consumption. However, loss of value due to unforeseen (unexpected) obsolescence, natural calamities (floods, fires and earthquakes), thefts etc. is not depreciation. It is called *capital loss*.

Annual depreciation allowance represents a charge against current year's production. Estimation of depreciation assumes significance because in a dynamic economy technological progress may necessitate the replacement of a fixed asset before the expiry of its physical life.

Depreciation estimation poses both conceptual and statistical problems. Depreciation is normally estimated on the basis of the expected life of the fixed capital and the interest rate, rather than on the basis of actual current capital consumption. It is very difficult to estimate correctly the life of a capital equipment. Wear and tear differs from machine to machine and from firm to firm. Therefore, it is calculated either as a fixed percentage of (a) gross value of output or (b) of invested capital. The second method, commonly used in business practice, yields more stable annual allowance.

In international trade, the term depreciation refers to the fall in the free market value of domestic currency in terms of foreign currencies.

Depression

It is a prolonged period of low economic activities with high unemployment in an economy. See also Great Depression.

Derivatives

Derivative instruments comprise financial products which have grown up around securities, currency and commodity trading and whose price is a function of some other underlying security, currency rate or other commodity. The term is usually used to include swaps, futures, options, forwards and a wide range of financially engineered instruments which are hybrids of other financial products.

Derived Demand See Final and Intermediate Products

Devaluation

As part of a government's commercial policy, it refers to deliberate reduction in the value of domestic currency in relation to foreign currencies. Devaluation makes domestically produced goods cheaper for the foreigners and foreign goods expensive for the locals. Hence, imports are reduced and exports are promoted to improve the trade balance. For successful devaluation, it is necessary that demand for imports as well as exports is relatively elastic.

Development Banks

Development banks are an important segment of the financial system of a country. These banks are specialised financial institutions which provide medium and long-term finance to private industry mainly large-scale industry. Some important development banks in India are: Industrial

Development Bank of India (IDBI), Industrial Finance Corporation of India (IFCI) and Industrial Credit and Investment Corporation of India (ICICI).

Industrial development banks perform various functions to promote economic development of a country.

1. They provide medium and long-term finance to industry. It is provided in the form of term loans and advances and subscription to shares and debentures.

2. They provide guarantees for term loans and underwrite new equity. Guarantees and underwriting by development banks create confidence among investors and thus facilitate raising of funds by companies.

3. Development banks perform various types of promotional roles for the private entrepreneurs as, for example, identification of investment projects, management services and technical advice.

Development banks are different from commercial banks in several respects. Firstly, development banks do not accept deposits from the public as commercial banks do. For example, financial resources of development banks in India come from Government of India, Reserve Bank of India and from international agencies like World Bank and its affiliate International Development Association.

Secondly, they specialise in providing medium-term and long-term finance while commercial banks generally provide short-term credit. Thirdly, development banks perform promotional role for industrial development of the country whereas commercial banks provide utility and other services to their customers.

Differential Rent **See Rent**

Dillion Round

It refers to tariff-reducing negotiations undertaken by GATT in 1961 among various contracting parties (member countries) and which were conducted on an across the board basis. It is dubbed so after the US Secretary of Treasury, Douglas Dillion.

Diminishing Marginal Rate of Substitution

When a consumer substitutes commodity X for commodity Y, the rate at which this substitution takes place is called the marginal rate of substitution. As he gets more and more of X he would be prepared to surrender less and less of Y. This is due to the operation of the law of diminishing marginal utility. The law of diminishing marginal rate of substitution is important because it explains why an Indifference Curve (q.v.) is convex to the origin.

Diminishing Marginal Utility, Law of **See Utility**

Diminishing Returns, Law of

Historically, the law of diminishing returns is associated with agricultural operations, with land being the fixed factor and labour the variable factor. However, this law holds good for all those productive activities where increasing quantities of a variable factor are applied to a given quantity of a fixed factor. Modern economists regard labour (L) and capital (K) to be the most significant factors of production, considering land as either unimportant or a part of capital.

The law of diminishing returns states that if increasing quantities of a variable factor (labour) are applied to a given quantity of fixed factor (land), the marginal product of the variable factor will eventually decline. The law is based on the following assumptions.

1. If one factor is kept fixed and increasing quantities of the other factor are applied, variations in the proportions of the two factors are implicitly assumed. This law will apply only to those cases where possibilities of variable proportions exist.

2. Since it is assumed that some factors are fixed therefore this law pertains to short-run.

3. Production technology is assumed to be given. A change in technology may postpone the operation of the law for sometime.

4. Different units of the variable factor are assumed to be homogenous.

Why does the law of diminishing returns hold good? There are valid explanations for the operation of this law. The marginal product increases in the first instance because increasing quantities of labour lead to division of labour and its advantages. In the beginning, the amount of labour is inadequate to utilise the fixed factor optimally and therefore there are increasing rather than decreasing returns. However, the scope for increasing returns must disappear eventually, i.e. marginal product of additional workers must decline. This is so because too many workers on the fixed factor will spoil the optimum ratio between land (fixed factor) and labour (variable factor). If the process of increasing the number of workers continues, they will start getting in each other's way and the marginal product may become zero or even negative. Were it not for the law of diminishing returns, the world food production could be raised on 1 hectare of land by simply increasing the quantity of labour on it.

Direct Tax

It is a tax the ultimate burden of which falls on the person on whom it is levied. In other words, it is a tax that cannot be shifted from the original payer to someone else. It is contrasted with Indirect Tax (q.v.) which can readily be shifted to ultimate consumers of the commodity or service taxed.

John Stuart Mill (1806-1873), the celebrated British economist of the 19th century, distinguished between direct and indirect taxes as follows. "A direct tax is one which is demanded from the very person who, it is intended or desired, should pay it. Indirect taxes are those which are demanded from one person in the expectation and intention that he shall indemnify himself at the expense of another."

Income tax, property tax and payroll tax are generally considered direct taxes, although many economists believe that it is possible to pass on these taxes under certain circumstances. Corporate income tax, a supposedly direct tax, is known to be shifted to consumers in many countries.

Direct taxes, though administratively inconvenient, are preferred because they

(a) can be related to ability-to-pay,
(b) satisfy the principle of certainty and
(c) create civic consciousness.

See also Indirect Tax; Tax Shifting; Incidence of Taxation; Statutory Incidence; and Economic Incidence.

Dirty Float See Managed Float

Discrete Variable See Variable

Discriminating Duty

An import duty levied at a level different from comparable import duties so as to encourage (or discourage) imports of a particular commodity or imports from a particular country. See also Commonwealth Preference; and Preferential Duty.

Discriminating Monopoly See Monopoly

Diseconomies of Scale See Returns to Scale

Disequilibrium

It is a situation of imbalance between opposing forces so that there is a tendency for change

Disguised Unemployment See Unemployment

Displacement Effect See Peacock-Wiseman Hypothesis

Dividend

It is the payment authorised by the board of directors of a company for pro rata distribution among the shares outstanding. On preference shares, it is generally a fixed amount. On common shares, the dividend varies with the fortunes of the company.

Dividend Cover

It is the ratio of the dividend paid to the net profit out of which it is paid.

Dividend to Price Ratio

It is the ratio of the dividend per share paid by a company to the market price of one share of that company. For example, a dividend of Rs. 1.50 per share with a market price of Rs. 30 gives a dividend yield of 1.50 / 30 x 100 = 5 per cent.

Division of Labour

There are two types of division of labour: (a) product-based division of labour and (b) process-based division of labour. If a worker specialises in the production of a single commodity or service, it is called product-based division of labour as, for example, a village cobbler. If a worker specialises in performing one or two of the several processes involved in the production of a commodity, it is called *process-based division* of labour as, for example, a worker working in a large shoe factory.

Division of labour has many advantages: (a) it increases the efficiency of labour, (b) it leads to the possibility of inventions and discoveries, (c) it saves time of the workers.

Domestic Factor Income

Income generated within the domestic territory of a country by all the producers is called domestic factor income. It is also called net value added at factor cost.

Domestic Savings

Savings represent the excess of current income over current expenditure of various sectors of the economy. For preparation of the estimates of domestic savings, the economy is divided into three broad institutional sectors: (a) public sector, (b) private corporate sector and (c) household sector. For a closed economy, savings equal capital formation during the year whereas for an open economy, savings equal capital formation plus net capital inflow from abroad during the year.

Domestic Territory of a Country

It includes: (a) territory lying within the political frontiers, (b) territorial waters of the country, (c) ships and aircrafts and (d) embassies of the country located abroad.

Double Taxation

It refers to the application of two separate taxes or tax systems to the same tax base, e.g. income.

Double taxation (or tax duplication) occurs when the same base is assessed twice either by the same tax jurisdiction or by two competing tax jurisdictions either at different levels of government in a country or at the same level of government in different countries. All the three versions of double taxation are described below.

A. Double Taxation by the Same Tax Jurisdiction: A common example of this kind of double taxation is the taxation of corporate earnings, first in the form of corporate income tax, and then in the form of personal income tax on dividends distributed to shareholders.

Tax laws usually contain provisions which mitigate or even eliminate tax duplication of this kind. Under one method, a shareholder is granted credit against his tax liability on overall income for the tax paid by the company on distributed profits. The credit may be granted on full or partial basis (say 50 per cent) on account of company tax on distributed profits.

B. Double Taxation by Competing Tax Jurisdictions at Different Levels of Government in a Country: Double taxation of this type arises when different levels of government impose taxes on the same base, e.g. taxation of income by Federal and State Governments in USA, and Canada.

C. Double Taxation by Competing Tax Jurisdictions at Same Level of Government in Different Countries: This kind of double taxation is also called international double taxation or territorial multiple taxation. In this case, two sovereign countries claim jurisdiction in taxing the same base, usually income.

Flow of labour and capital from one country to another is common. Multinationals operate in a number of countries, and individual investors possess internationally diversified investment portfolios. Thus, companies and individuals receive foreign income in the form of profits, dividends and royalties.

Tax problems associated with international flow of labour and capital are complex. International community has devised some rules to minimise/eliminate international tax duplication so that international flow of labour and capital is not unduly obstructed.

Two fundamental assignment rules govern the right of nations to impose taxes on foreign income: (a) source rule (or territoriality rule) and (b) residence rule (or domicile rule).

Source rule holds that income ought to be taxed in the country in which it originates irrespective of whether the income accrues to a resident or a non-resident assessee. The claim for tax jurisdiction is made on the ground that source country allows non-residents to use its infrastructure and other inputs for production purposes and therefore it can legitimately take a bite into their earnings.

According to the residence rule, the power to tax foreign income should belong to the country in which the taxpayer resides. The tests of residence including nationality of individual assessees are complex and vary from country to country. Similarly, different countries follow different rules to define a domestic/foreign company. The claim of the residence (or home) country rests on the ground that the source (or host) country utilises and benefits from manpower and other resources trained and perfected by the home country.

Problem of international tax duplication can be avoided if all the countries follow either the source or the residence rule. In practice, most countries exercise source and residence rules concurrently. If a country observes only the residence rule, then it surrenders tax claim on incomes which originate within its political jurisdiction and accrue to non-residents. A country would normally not go for this option which favours the foreigners vis-a-vis its own citizens. In most cases, countries tax their residents on their world income, and the non-residents on their incomes originating within their borders. International tax duplication arises when the country of residence extends the tax net to the world income of a taxpayer and the host country follows the source rule. Double taxation of this kind discourages international movement of factors of production.

Methods to Alleviate International Double Taxation: Various procedures may be followed by concerned countries to reduce or even eliminate double taxation of foreign-source income of their residents.

A. ***Exemption Method:*** A country may voluntarily and unilaterally sacrifice its tax claim on the foreign income of its residents. In other words, foreign income of residents is exempt from taxation in the home country. For example, there is no further tax on repatriated profits in countries such as France, and Germany.

B. Foreign Tax Credit: The home country permits deduction of taxes paid by the residents in the host country (on dividends, royalties etc.) from the tax on world-wide income due in the home country. The foreign tax credit is a mechanism provided unilaterally by a number of countries to alleviate the effect of double taxation. The object is to reduce tax on foreign-source income to the extent that income has already been taxed in the foreign jurisdiction.

A foreign tax credit system was introduced in Australia on July 1, 1987. Under this system, the foreign-source income of residents is taxed at normal rates in Australia, with a credit granted for the foreign taxes paid. Other important countries which operate a tax credit mechanism as a means of eliminating double taxation are USA, UK, Canada, and Japan.

C. Lenient Tax Treatment: A country may treat foreign-source income leniently (by applying a lower rate of tax) than domestic income. Such discriminatory treatment in favour of foreign income will reduce but not eliminate tax duplication.

D. Bilateral Agreements: International double taxation is also avoided through bilateral tax treaties. See also Double Tax Treaty.

Double Taxation Relief

It is an arrangement to prevent the same income from being taxed twice, particularly when a shareholder and a company are domiciled in different countries. See also Double Taxation.

Double Tax Treaty

It means a convention or an agreement among countries for the avoidance of double taxation of income and capital and bringing uniformity in the allocation of taxation rights in cross-border situations. It is essentially a bargain between two treaty countries as regards the division of tax revenue between them in respect of income falling to be taxed in both jurisdictions. Since treaty negotiations involve bargaining, each side seeks concessions from the other and it is not necessary that strict *quid pro quo* is achieved at the end.

Apart from relieving double taxation, a double tax treaty aids commercial relations between treaty partners. It creates an environment of fiscal certainty which encourages trade and investment between countries. It provides rules for resolving problems of dual residence or dual source of income, defines the different forms of taxable income and determines the taxing rights of the two treaty countries. An important provision of all double tax treaties is the machinery for administrative co-operation between the tax authorities of treaty partners.

Advantages and disadvantages of a double tax treaty depend on the flow of trade and investment between treaty partners. If these flows are in balance, which is a rarity, the benefits and costs would be truly reciprocal. Where the flows of trade and investment are unbalanced, the advantages of the treaty may be weighed more in favour of one treaty partner than the other, though the provisions of the treaty may be expressed in reciprocal terms. This is generally the case regarding tax treaties between developed and underdeveloped countries where flows of trade and investment are one-sided.

Multilateral Double Tax Conventions: Multilateral double tax treaties, though considered at different times in various contexts, have not gained acceptance for being complex. It is difficult to understand and apply a multilateral treaty than a bilateral one. Moreover, a multilateral convention is less flexible in terms of amendment, revision, or termination.

Though multilateral approach is not generally followed, there are, at least, three notable multilateral double income tax agreements. 1. **Andean Pact.** This agreement among the member states of Andean Group (Bolivia, Chile, Columbia, Ecuador, Peru, and Venezuela) is based on the principle of giving the state of source the exclusive right of taxation. 2. **Comecon Conventions.** There are two multilateral agreements for the avoidance of double taxation among 8 of the 10 member states of Comecon (Bulgaria, Czechoslovakia, erstwhile GDR, Hungary, Mongolia, Poland, Romania, erstwhile U.S.S.R, Cuba, and Vietnam). The last two are not signatories to the multilateral agreements. 3. **Nordic Countries**. A multilateral treaty covering tax on income and capital exists among Nordic countries (Denmark, Finland, Iceland, Norway, and Sweden).

Bilateral Double Tax Conventions: Most tax treaties are bilateral. Some international organisations have done commendable work in the development and harmonisation of bilateral double tax conventions. Model tax treaties drawn up by these organisations have helped to harmonise national approaches to double tax relief. They have facilitated the negotiation of tax treaties by eliminating the need for elaborate analysis and protracted discussion of every issue involved in each treaty.

OECD Model Conventions: In 1963, OECD published a Draft Double Taxation Convention. In 1977, it issued a Model Double Taxation Convention based on the experience of OECD member states since 1963. The OECD Model gives the primary right of taxation to the state of residence. It operates largely in favour of the developed capital exporting countries, and to the consequent detriment of underdeveloped countries which are net importers of foreign investment.

In 1966, OECD issued a draft convention on estates and inheritances. In 1982, it published a revised version of the same which included gifts also. The OECD conventions have been widely accepted among OECD member states and other developed countries.

United Nations Model Convention, 1980: United Nations adopted a resolution in 1967 to constitute a group of experts on tax treaties between developed and developing countries. Special problems arise where a double tax treaty is concluded between developed and developing countries. Based on the report of the group of experts, the United Nations issued in 1979 a Manual for tax treaty negotiators. In 1980, it issued its Model Double Taxation Convention Between Developed and Developing Countries.

The basic difference between the United Nations model and the OECD model is that the former predominantly gives the source country the right to tax income while the latter grants the country of residence the right to tax income. United Nations model is generally used when one of the countries is a developing one. This is so because normally investments flow from a developed country to a developing country which *ipso facto* means that incomes flow from developing to developed countries, i.e. developing countries are the source of income. See also Tax Treaty Shopping.

Dual Exchange Market

It is a foreign exchange market in which citizens who require foreign currency to purchase foreign goods must buy it at the commercial (the pegged) exchange rate while citizens who wish to buy and sell financial assets must use the floating rate of exchange.

This type of market is a special case of multiple exchange market and is often prevalent in developing countries, or where foreign exchange is scarce.

Dummy Variable See Variable

Dumping

It is a practice of selling goods in a foreign country at a price below their domestic selling price, after allowing for differences due to transportation expenses, tariffs, and other cost justifications. Many governments view the activity as an unfair competitive practice and frequently expose those engaged in dumping to the imposition of an antidumping duty. This generally unfavourable view of the practice stems from the monopoly precondition which underlies it. Economic theory specifies that in order for a producer to discriminate in the pricing of identical goods between markets (or classes of consumers) some element of monopoly power must be present; otherwise, the producer is merely a price-taker forced to adopt the uniform competitive price determined in the overall marketplace.

Conditions for successful dumping: For successful international dumping, the following conditions need to be satisfied.

1. The home and foreign markets are sufficiently separated to prevent arbitrage by foreign buyers in such a way that the cheap dumped goods cannot be resold by foreign buyers in the original market at a price which undercuts the domestic monopoly price.

2. There exists less competition in the home market than the foreign market, making foreign customers more responsive to an individual producer's price changes than domestic customers. Under these circumstances, the incentive for a producer to engage in international dumping is explained by the broader concept and theory of third-degree price discrimination, of which dumping is really a special case.

A producer interested in maximising profits given these conditions should price goods in different geographical locations so that the marginal revenue received from the last unit of those goods sold is equal in all locations, and at the same time equal to the overall marginal cost of production of those goods. If it is assumed that there is no difference in costs between markets and the revenue the producer receives from selling an additional unit of goods in the foreign market exceeds that received from the last unit sold in the home market, it is more profitable to lower the foreign price in order to sell another unit there and to raise the domestic price in order to sell a unit less at home. The incentive to reprice continues until the marginal revenues from each market are equilibrated to each other as well as to marginal cost of production. Where foreign market demand facing the producer is more responsive to price changes than domestic market demand, and where arbitrage cannot occur, this profit-maximising formula will ultimately result in a situation where the producer is motivated to price goods in the foreign market more cheaply than at home.

Dunnage

It refers to packing material of various kinds (straw, glass fibre etc.) used to keep goods from being damaged while in a ship's hold

Duopoly

Duopoly is a market situation characterised by two sellers and many buyers. Duopoly (or Cournot's equilibrium) is the simplest and special case of oligopoly. Since in duopoly there are only two producers, any price or output change by one is bound to affect the other significantly. Among the various models for the behaviour of a duopolist firm, the one given by the French economist A. A. Cournot (1801-1877) is the most widely accepted.

Cournot's equilibrium assumes that there are two firms selling identical product (e.g. spring water) under conditions of zero cost of production. Therefore, the profit-maximising level of sales of each firm occurs at the mid-point of its negatively sloped straight line demand curve, where elasticity of demand is one, marginal revenue is zero and total revenue is maximum. See also Duopsony.

Duopsony

It is a market situation in which there are only two buyers of a particular commodity or service. See also Duopoly.

Durable and Non-durable Goods

All goods produced can be divided into two categories: (a) Durable goods, i.e. goods which can be used over and over again for a number of years. Their expected life time of use is more than one year as, for example, machines and buildings. (b) Non-durable goods are those which cannot be used more than once. The moment they are used they lose their identity as, for example, milk, bread and services of all types.

Duty Drawback

It refers to repayment of import duty, partially or fully, to exporters of commodities in the manufacture of which imported materials and components are used. Duty drawback scheme is a device to encourage exports. Most often, the scheme is used for imported raw materials or semi-finished goods (like raw diamonds) that are incorporated into a finished product (cut and polished diamonds) and then re-exported.

Complications arise when exported goods use raw materials and components some of which are imported and some produced domestically. The drawback in such cases means refund of an amount which represents the import duty paid on the imported materials used in the exported goods.

Duty-free Shop

A shop at airports, on ships etc. from where outgoing passengers may buy goods which are free of commodity taxes because the purchases are meant for exports. Similarly, incoming passengers may purchase certain goods from duty-free shop at a cheaper price than usual because they do not have to pay duty that is usually paid when goods are brought into a country.

Duty-free Zone **See Free Port**

Dynamic Theory of Profit **See Profit**

E

Earmarking of Taxes

Earmarking is a fiscal practice under which revenues from one or more sources are pooled into a separate independent fund which is used to finance certain pre-determined public services.

The purpose of earmarking is to ensure stable funding for important public activities. Another objective of earmarking is to introduce market prices into the budgetary process. In this sense, earmarked taxes become indirect form of market prices charged for public services rendered.

Among the conditions for successful earmarking, the following are more important. 1. There should be a clear-cut linkage between the tax levied and the benefit received. 2. Expenditure is well-defined so that the taxpayers can identify its obvious benefits. 3. Linkage between earmarked revenue (e.g. from motor vehicle tax) and pre-determined expenditure (e.g. on construction and maintenance of municipal roads and bridges) is tight. 4. Revenue is in the form of direct user charge/benefit tax (e.g. a toll).

Traditionally, financing of road expenditure from out of tolls, motor vehicle taxes and fuel taxes has been considered an area with a strong economic rationale for earmarking. Similarly, airport tax is generally levied to meet expenditure on airport maintenance. The principle of earmarking could be applied to such municipal services as water supply and sewage disposal by linking them to water and sewer charges which, in many cases, are components of the property tax in the sense that the base for these charges is the same as used for property (e.g. annual rental value). The principle of earmarking should not be applied indiscriminately because too many funds created under it would be difficult to control.

Earned and Unearned Income

Earned income (or employment or labour income) is derived from actual work or services performed and includes wages, salaries and income from professions. Unearned income (or capital or property income) is derived from investment, rent etc.

Should tax laws distinguish between earned and unearned income in order to accord a favourable treatment to the former? Lenient treatment of earned income is justified on various grounds. Employment earnings represent returns on current efforts whereas capital income is often the result of inherited wealth, monopoly power, capital gains, gambling wins and property received through gifts and marriages.

Earned income is more uncertain than investment income. A human being is a depreciating asset which ceases to earn on retirement or death. Uncertainty of the human asset also arises from possible chances of suspension, dismissal, premature retirement from service, illness, unemployment and accident. Contrarily, physical and financial assets have a tendency to appreciate in value with the passage of time, particularly in a growing economy. Uncertainties associated with business income are less grievous and can be insured against by making gilt-edged investments.

Possession of property, besides being a source of monetary return, confers certain other benefits on the possessor, e.g. ability to dissave, security and independence.

It may also be argued that expenditure incurred in connection with earning income from employment (including expenses on education and training) is far more than that incurred in obtaining investment income. Therefore, it is unjust to treat the fruits of one's own labour and windfall profits equally.

J.E. Meade Committee Report on *The Structure and Reform of Direct Taxation* advanced the following four arguments as to why earned income should be treated *softly* vis-a-vis other income for tax purposes. 1. Earned income is less permanent than investment income. 2. Earned income involves a sacrifice of leisure which is absent in the case of income from property, particularly from inherited property. 3. Earned income is the creation of a taxpayer's own skill, ability, and effort while unearned income may accrue through the luck of inheritance. 4. Prestige, security, independence and influence, generally associated with the ownership of wealth, are absent in the case of earned income.

It is also well-known that labour earnings are recorded more systematically and in most cases tax is deducted at source, leaving no scope for malpractice in tax payment. As Vito Tanzi has observed, "Income taxes on wages and salaries cannot be evaded, or at least it is much harder to do so, which provides a good ground for a lighter treatment of these incomes. In fact, if they are treated in the same way as other incomes, and if the assumption is true that taxes on them are difficult to evade, then a *de jure* non-discriminatory treatment of these incomes would amount to a *de facto* discrimination."

It is not surprising that tax laws of many countries provide for relatively lenient tax treatment of earned income, e.g. earned income tax credit in the USA.

Some economists argue that the distinction between earned and unearned income is misleading because to the extent that property embodies past labour, the income from it is not *unearned* and should not be taxed at a higher rate than earned income.

Earning Per Share

It means profit over a given period, reduced by preference dividend, divided by the number of shares outstanding at the end of that period.

Earning to Price Ratio

It is the ratio of the Earning Per Share (q.v.) of a company to the market price of one share of that company.

East Asian Crisis

In their desire to attract large amount of foreign capital, some East Asian countries (notably Indonesia) allowed domestic banks and companies to borrow freely in the world financial markets under open capital account. This led to large-scale accumulation of short-term external debt. Banks and other financial intermediaries in these countries were not proficient enough to handle sudden inflow of massive volumes of foreign capital. A sizeable proportion of these funds was diverted to unproductive channels, e.g. investments in real estates. Poor financial intermediation, unimaginative utilisation and change in lenders' perception about borrowers' capabilities led to massive and sudden outflow of funds from these countries, creating a currency crisis with crippling effects on these economies.

The disastrous experience of East Asian countries has deterred developing countries like India to liberalise their capital account.

East India Company

A British company chartered in 1600 by Queen Elizabeth I. It held a position of dominance as the world's largest and most powerful company for nearly 200 years. It ruled over a large part of Bengal, Bihar, Orissa and the United Provinces till British government took over them in 1858.

Econometrics

As a branch of economics, econometrics deals with the empirical measurement of economic relations that are expressible in mathematical form.

Economic and Non-economic Resources

Economics is a social science concerned with the administration of scarce resources. Resources are of two types: (a) economic resources and (b) non-economic resources. Economic resources like labour, capital, equipment and land are limited or scarce. They command a price. Contrarily, non-economic resources such as sunshine and air are unlimited in supply and therefore available free of cost. Economics deals with scarce resources.

Economic Development See Economic Growth and Economic Development

Economic Dualism

Economic dualism, a characteristic feature of most less developed countries (LDCs) of the world, means the coexistence of a modern industrial sector and a traditional agricultural sector in an economy. Dualism in LDCs is the result of colonial domination. Historically, dualism crept into these countries when the colonial powers introduced a modern sector into the traditional economies of subjugated countries.

A dual economy is characterised by surplus labour in the subsistence agricultural sector. By expanding the modern sector through transfer of surplus labour from the traditional sector, economic development can be speeded up in LDCs. Given the sectoral differential in productivity of modern sector and traditional sector, transfer of labour from the latter to the former will be a step towards sectoral productivity equalisation. Through this process, economic dualism is overcome and the economy is said to be integrated. Hence, growth with mployment is achieved.

Let us divide an underdeveloped economy into modern (M) sector and a traditional (T) sector. The economic development of this economy involves the process of surplus labour transfer from the traditional sector to the modern sector. The speed of labour transfer is determined by the rate of industrial investment and capital accumulation in the modern sector.

The traditional sector is non-capitalist. It is self-employment sector with massive surplus labour or disguised unemployment. The modern sector is capitalist, using reproducible capital.

The process starts when demand for industrial goods expands autonomously, may be due to foreign markets.

Consequently, the derived demand for labour increases. As a result, workers move from agriculture to industry. Abundant labour supply at the existing wage rate keep labour cost of the industries low. Meanwhile, rising demand and higher industrial prices lead to greater profits. When these profits are reinvested for capital formation, the demand for industrial output rises in two categories: (a) consumption goods demanded by newly employed workers and (b) capital goods demanded by owners of capital.

Rising demand for industrial production leads to further shift of labour out of agriculture into industry. As the shift from agriculture to industry proceeds, agricultural productivity rises while the number of farmers fall. Labour migration would stop when the point of equal attraction is reached, i.e. when the marginal product of labour in the two sectors is equal. See also Technological Dualism.

Economic Growth and Economic Development

Strictly speaking, economic growth and economic development are not interchangeable terms. Economic growth is narrower in concept and means sustained increase in per capita real income. Two conditions need to be satisfied for this to happen. 1. An increase in national income at current prices does not necessarily mean increase in output because such an increase may be due to rising prices. Hence, the first condition is that increase in national income should be real, i.e. in terms of constant prices. In other words, money national income should be subjected to GNP deflator to remove the spurious effect of inflation. 2. If mass poverty in a country is to be removed, the emphasis must be on increase in per capita real income rather than simply on increase in the country's real national income. For this purpose, the population variable has to be considered. Clearly, if real national income and population increase at the same rate, the per capita real income will remain the same. For the per capita real income to increase, it is necessary that the rate of increase in real national income is more than proportionate to the rate of increase in population.

Economic development is a much wider term. It includes economic growth and at the same time encompasses questions regarding pattern of production, distribution of income and consumption behaviour of the people. In other words, economic development is economic growth plus qualitative changes in productivity, socio-economic institutions and distribution pattern.

Determinants of economic development in a country include the following: availability of natural resources, proportion of current income devoted to capital formation, capital-output ratio, occupational structure, growth of population and technological progress.

Economic Imperialism

In pre-capitalist societies, economic expansionism was irregular, unsystematic and not an integral part of normal economic activity. Economic gains from expansion were windfall gains, frequently taking the form of plunder. Plunder acquired in the course of expansion was often consumed in the field by the conquering armies, leaving the home economy relatively unaffected.

Industrial capitalist expansion (or *neo-mercantilism*) was a feature of 19th century and early 20th century. It exhibited a more aggressive attitude towards the underexploited lands. It was less particular, and more universal in character. It more fully integrated underexploited economic regions into the structure of the metropolitan country. Moreover, it required the active participation of the state.

According to Marxists, economic imperialism depends on colonial rule. Thus, political independence would significantly reduce, or eliminate entirely, exploitative imperialist relations. However, Marxists have been forced to do rethinking on this question in view of the current domination of USA in the world without actually occupying territories.

The phrase *neo-colonialism* (i.e. modern imperialism) was first used in the early 1950s. The chief manifestations of neo-colonialism are the following: (a) puppet governments represented by stooges who, in most cases, are unpopular politicians, corrupt civil or military functionaries, (b) continuity of economic dependence after formal recognition of national sovereignty, (c) economic infiltration by a foreign power after independence through capital investments, loans, grants or technical experts, (d) military bases, sometimes introduced as scientific research stations or training schools.

Neo-colonialism is the survival of the colonial system in spite of formal recognition of political independence in emerging countries. Neo-colonialism requires the active participation of the state in international economic relations. More dangerously, the neo-colonist policy is first and foremost designed to prevent the newly independent countries from consolidating their political independence.

Economic domination by the developed countries takes the form of control over the liquid and real economic resources of backward countries. Liquid resources are foreign exchange and savings while real resources consist of agricultural and mineral assets and facilities like transportation and communication.

Modern imperialism adopts informal, rather than formal, control over backward countries. The use of old economic and political ties is practised wherever possible as, for example, the relationship formed within the British Commonwealth. Direct colonial rule has been replaced by military alliances, economic and cultural missions and bribes to local ruling classes. Only when indirect policies fail are the older instruments of coercion and force brought into play. Direct involvement of USA in the recent Gulf war is a case in point.

Economic Laws

As a social science, economics deals with human behaviour, i.e. behaviour of human beings as consumers and producers. An economic law is a statement that has been successfully tested again and again. Since human behaviour is not accurately predictable, the laws of economics are not as exact as those of physical sciences. British economist Alfred Marshall (1842-1924), compared economic laws with the law of tides rather than the law of gravitation which states exactly the force with which a thing falls to the ground.

Economic Models

An economic model is a statement of relationship among economic variables. It is used to explain the cause and effect relationship among variables. Economic models are helpful in explaining and predicting economic phenomena as, for example, cost behaviour of firms. Aggregate models deal with the economy as a whole. Sectoral models examine particular sectors of the economy like industry or agriculture. Inter-industry models explain relationship among various industries using input-output matrices.

Economic Rent **See Rent**

Economics

It is a social science concerned with the study of production, distribution, exchange and consumption of goods and services.

Economic Sanctions

They refer to measures taken by a country/group of countries to persuade/pressurise another country to follow a certain course of action. Economic sanctions generally take the form of suspension of financial assistance and restrictions on exports to and imports from the country to be penalised.

Economic System

An economic system is a man-made device designed to facilitate the use of resources and the distribution of output. It consists of a complex set of institutions, laws and objectives. Every economy has to accomplish certain basic tasks. These are: (a) allocation of resources among competing uses, (b) choice of technology and (c) distribution of output.

Which is the best economic system? It is difficult to answer this question because it involves subjective preferences about welfare, progress, freedom and security. Still, attempts can be made to evaluate economic systems on certain rational criteria.

The first thing one would like to know about economies with different economic systems is how much they produce. The measure of production can be national income disaggregated into industrial and agricultural output, or into private goods and collective goods. Per capita real income would still be a better index.

However, there are limitations of this criterion. Lower per capita income of a country does not necessarily mean that its economic system is inferior. In fact, a country's per capita income depends not only on its economic institutions but also on historical, political, cultural, geographical and social circumstances as well.

Rate of growth is an important criterion of successful economic performance. In most underdeveloped countries economic growth constitutes the major national objective and the success of the government is largely measured in terms of the rate of growth in national income. However, it would be wrong to assume that growth alone can solve social and economic problems. Moreover, economic growth has contributed to the deterioration of the environment, as most industrialised societies have discovered to their sorrow. Some other criteria to judge the performance of different economic systems include: (a) economic stability, (b) individual's economic security, (c) equity and justice and (d) economic freedom.

Economic Union

It is the highest form of economic integration among different countries having the following features: (a) no tariff restrictions on intra-union trade, (b) common tariff rates for imports from non-members, (c) free movement of factors of production within the union and (d) harmonious monetary, fiscal and tax policies of the member countries.

Economic Welfare

Increase in per capita real income is the conventional definition of economic growth. However, this definition cannot be used to mean increase in economic welfare. Apart from increase in per capita real income, there are additional considerations which must be taken into account before judgement is passed regarding increase in economic welfare. Per capita real income is just a partial index of economic welfare.

While a sustained increase in per capita real income should be the primary goal, this should be qualified in terms of a number of subgoals. The sustained increase in per capita real income should be accompanied by a decrease in economic inequalities and in the absolute number of people below the poverty line. Growing disparities increase the welfare of a small section of the population. Thus, the degree of inequality and how it has changed with increase in national income is of crucial importance.

Another relevant factor is the composition of total output that gives rise to increase in per capita real income. The quality of output-mix is as important as its quantity. If a great deal of production consists of war goods or other injurious items like cigarettes and liquor, national income will not reflect economic welfare. However, instead of tanks and missiles if a larger part of national income is composed of textiles, sugar, milk and other wage goods, it will indicate enhanced economic well-being of the people.

Modern production process involves pollution of air, water and calmness, reducing welfare of the people.

Similarly, certain expenditures of the government as, for example, on defence and control of riots do not add to economic welfare. These expenditures though necessary are unproductive.. These items, called *regrettable costs,* ought to be deducted from national income in order to arrive at a true measure of economic welfare.

Similarly, the process of sustained increase in per capita real income needs to be tested against achievements on other fronts such as specified minimum level of consumption, maximum level of tolerance unemployment, avoidance of marked interregional disparities and diversification of the economy.

Thus, to say that economic welfare has increased just because per capita real income has increased is wrong. It follows from above that increase in per capita real income is a necessary but not a sufficient condition for increase in economic welfare.

Economies of Scale See Returns to Scale

Effective Rate of Protection (ERP)

It refers to the real rate of protection given to internal commodities which may be import substitutes. Suppose cloth import is subject to a nominal 10 per cent tariff but raw cotton is imported free. If raw cotton is 50 per cent of cloth's final value then it means value added of the cloth manufacturing is also 50 per cent. Hence a 10 per cent tax on cloth really means an effective 20 per cent tax on value added (because raw cotton import is free). It is for this reason that nominal tariff does not reflect adequately the real protection which is done by ERP.

Effects of Taxes

Taxes affect economic behaviour of individuals and organisations in several ways. They affect our decisions regarding savings, investments, location of production centres, techniques of production, and above all consumption of different goods.

All taxes involve money burden on the people. Total yield of a tax to a government indicates total direct money burden on the citizens. Taxes also generate indirect money burden. For example, excise duty is collected by the government from the producer who in turn recovers it from the consumers. There is generally a time gap between the payment of excise by the producer and its subsequent recovery from the consumers. The lock up of money during this period devolves on the producer an indirect money burden which is equal to the interest he could have earned on that money.

Similarly, a distinction is drawn between direct and indirect real burden of a tax. According to Hugh Dalton, "To part with a shilling in payment of a tax means a greater sacrifice of economic welfare for a poor man than for a rich man. But that is a question, not of the incidence, but of the direct real burden of the tax. Again, when the price of sugar is raised by taxation, a family may have to eat less sugar, and so make a sacrifice of economic welfare. But that is a question, not of the incidence, but of the indirect real burden of the tax."

By distorting consumption patterns, taxes may lead to inefficient use of resources. Taxes also affect the relative economic positions of individuals and households.

Elasticity of Demand

The demand for a commodity is determined mainly by the price of the commodity. Also, demand is inversely related to the price of the commodity. This relationship is qualitative in nature, i.e. it speaks only of the direction of change. Apart from the direction of change, economists also want to know the magnitude of change. To quantify the change, they use the concept of price elasticity of demand or simply elasticity of demand.

Elasticity of demand establishes quantitative relationship between demand and price of a commodity. A change in price evokes a change in quantity demanded. Elasticity of demand is a technique to measure the responsiveness of demand to price changes. It compares the percentage change in price with the percentage change in quantity demanded. More specifically, elasticity of demand is the ratio of percentage change in demand to percentage change in price. The formula is:

$$\text{Elasticity of demand} = \frac{\text{\%age change in quantity demanded}}{\text{\%age change in price}}$$

Reaction of demand to price changes is not the same in all cases. In some cases, a small reduction in price may produce a large increase in quantity demanded while in some other cases, demand may remain insensitive to price changes. In other words, the sensitivity of demand to price changes is different for different commodities. In fact, the range of demand elasticity can be classified into the following five categories:

1. Completely Elastic Demand: It is an extreme situation in which a change in price leads to infinite change in demand. It is difficult to give example of a commodity the demand for which is completely elastic. This case represents a theoretical possibility.

2. Relatively Elastic Demand: When the percentage change in demand exceeds percentage change in price, the demand is said to be relatively elastic, i.e. its coefficient is more than 1. If a 10 per cent decrease in the price of sugar leads to a 20 per cent increase in its demand, the demand will be termed relatively elastic, the value of elasticity coefficient being 2.

3. Unitary Elastic Demand: When the percentage change in demand is equal to percentage change in price, the demand is said to be unitary elastic. If the price of sugar decreases by 20 per cent and demand increases by 20 per cent, the elasticity coefficient is 1, representing a moderate situation.

4. Relatively Inelastic Demand: If the percentage change in demand is less than the percentage change in price, the value of elasticity coefficient is less than 1 and the demand is said to be relatively inelastic.

5. Completely Inelastic Demand: This is another extreme situation depicting complete insensitivity of demand to price changes. In other words, change in price leads to no change in demand.

Determinants of Elasticity of Demand: Why is elasticity of demand more for some goods and less for others? This is so due to a host of factors.

1. Nature of the Commodity: In our daily life we consume many things. Some of these are absolutely essential for our survival as, for example, cereals, sugar and milk. These necessities of life have to be purchased whether their prices go up or down. Therefore, the demand for these goods is relatively inelastic. In other words, price variations exert little influence on the demand for essentials of life. As against these, we also buy commodities which are for our comfort or luxury consumption such as ice-cream, video tapes, furniture and cosmetics. If prices of comforts and luxuries increase too much, we can dispense with their consumption. Hence, price variations cause considerable influence on demand, i.e. demand is relatively elastic.

2. Number and Closeness of Substitutes: The extent to which substitutes of a given commodity are available also affects the elasticity of demand. For example, there are good substitutes for tea in the form of coffee and cocoa. When the price of tea increases, consumers readily switch over to these substitutes. Therefore, the demand elasticity for tea is likely to be high. Conversely, there are commodities for which close substitutes are not available as, for example, sugar. When the price of sugar increases, we cannot easily switch over to its substitutes. Generally, the demand for commodities with poor substitutes is inelastic.

3. Number of Uses: There are commodities which can be put to a number of uses such as electricity, aluminium and milk. If the prices of such commodities are high, we use them for very essential purposes. However, when prices decline, we start using them for relatively non-essential purposes also. Apparently, the demand for such commodities is relatively elastic. Conversely, butter is used as a food item only and therefore its demand is likely to be inelastic.

4. Proportion of Income Spent: In real life, we purchase commodities which have very low prices. Thus, we spend a very small proportion of our income on commodities like buttons, needles and match boxes. Even if the price of such commodities is doubled, we continue to buy them in the same quantity. Hence, the demand for such commodities is relatively inelastic.

5. ***Habit Forming Commodities:*** There are commodities the consumption of which becomes habit for some people as, for example, cigarette smoking. Increase in the price of cigarettes hardly affects the demand of the smokers. Since the demand is unresponsive to price changes therefore it is inelastic.

Apart from its theoretical significance, the concept of elasticity has practical applications. Information about the elasticity of demand for their products helps the producers to undertake successful price variations. If the demand is elastic, producers will be cautious while contemplating price increase.

For a successful tax policy, it is necessary to take into account the elasticity of demand of the taxed commodity. For example, excessive excise duty on a luxury item (say motor car) will not necessarily mean more revenue for the government. However, taxation of necessities is always revenue productive.

In the field of international trade, elasticity of demand is a major factor in determining terms of trade. Countries exporting goods with inelastic demand are better placed to influence terms of trade. This is one reason why petroleum exporting countries in the middle-east have often dictated world prices of petroleum products. In the context of international trade, devaluation of currency by a country will be successful only if its exports and imports are elastic. If exports and imports are inelastic, devaluation of the currency will not be effective in improving the balance of payment position.

Elasticity of Supply

The law of supply establishes direct relationship between price and the supply of a commodity. It does not speak of the quantification of this relationship. To measure the degree of relationship between the price and supply of a commodity, the concept of elasticity of supply is used. The elasticity of supply measures the reaction of supply to changes in price. More precisely, elasticity of supply is the ratio of percentage change in supply to percentage change in price. Symbolically,

$$Es = \frac{\%\text{age change in quantity supplied}}{\%\text{age change in price}}$$

Elasticity of Tax Revenue **See Buoyancy and Elasticity of Tax Revenue**

Embargo

It is an official order that restricts/forbids trade, movement of ships etc with other country/countries.

Enclave Theory

Trade makes a poor economy a dualist one in which there emerges an export-oriented developed sector or an enclave which has higher earnings (from exports) than the rest of the economy which remains generally poor.

End-use Classification of Goods

All the goods and services produced can be grouped into the following three categories depending on the use to which they are put: (a) Goods, both durable and non-durable (including services), which are used for consumption purpose are called *consumer goods*. (b) Goods and services used for producing other goods and services are *intermediate goods*. (c) Durable goods (machines, buildings etc.) used in the production process are called *capital goods*. Stocks of raw materials, semi-finished and finished goods lying with the producers at the end of the accounting year are also a part of capital goods.

Engel's Law

Named after German Statistician Ernst Engel (1821-1896), this law states proportions of income spent on goods and services by different income groups in a country. It states that as income of a family increases, a smaller and smaller proportion of it is spent on food.

Entertainment Tax

It is levied on the price charged for admission to various places of entertainment such as a cinema, circus, theatre, exhibition, variety show, cabaret, night-club and casino.

Equal Product Curve **See Isoquant Curve**

Equation of Exchange

It is an explanation for price level changes which cause changes in the value of money. In fact, price level is a matter of relationship between money and the goods which it is used to buy.

Money in an economy consists partly of currency and partly of bank deposits. The currency and bank deposits that actually circulate are used over and over again in the course of a specified period (say one year). Every time they are used they enter into a price. Therefore, the total amount of purchasing power which enters into the price level depends on the flow (rather than the stock) of money. The flow can be considered in terms of the stock if the latter is multiplied by its velocity of circulation which is defined as the average number of times a unit of money changes hands during the course of one year. If M is the stock of money and V its velocity of circulation, then the flow of money will be MV.

On the other hand, there are goods and services that are exchanged against money. In fact, every time there is a business transaction in which any commodity or service is offered in exchange for money, a price emerges that enters into the price level. Furthermore, if a given commodity passes through several hands, a price is established at each such transfer. In other words, this commodity enters into the price level several times. Hence, the commodity side of the price level consists of the total number of units exchanged in a given period of time (one year). These units can be represented by the letter T, i.e. total number of unit transactions, or the total volume of trade.

Algebraically, average price in all these transactions must be equal to the total flow of money divided by the number of goods exchanged. If we represent this average price by P, then we have the simple algebraic formula: $P = MV / T$. This formula is known as the equation of exchange.

It is clear from this equation that the value of P must depend upon the ratio between the numerator and the denominator. Or, to put it differently, the general level of prices must depend upon the ratio between the flow of money (MV) and the flow of goods (T). When more money is spent relatively to the goods flowing into the markets, prices can be expected to rise. Conversely, if the flow of money is reduced, goods remaining unchanged, prices can be expected to fall. Similarly, if the flow of goods increases in relation to the flow of money, prices will fall, and if flow of goods decreases, money in circulation remaining unchanged, prices will rise. Equation of exchange is one version of the quantity theory of money.

Equilibrium

It is a situation of balance between opposing forces so that there is no tendency for change.

Equilibrium Price

Equilibrium price is a situation in which the quantity of a product supplied and the quantity demand are equal. An equilibrium price is one at which the quantity decisions of buyers and sellers exactly satisfy each other. Geometrically, equilibrium occurs at the intersection of market demand curve and market supply curve of a commodity. At the equilibrium point there is neither a surplus nor a shortage of the commodity and the market clears itself. In such a situation there is no market force leading to a price change unless the non-price determinants of supply and demand are altered. It is possible that the price deviates from the equilibrium point temporarily. If this happens, then the operation of market forces will bring back the price to equilibrium point.

Equi-marginal Utility, Law of **See Utility**

Escape Clause

This clause is inserted in foreign trade agreements for providing a right to withdraw some given concessions if they threaten a serious disadvantage to domestic competitors.

Estate Duty

It is a levy on the value of the entire estate left behind by a decedent before its division among the inheritors. It is contrasted with an Inheritance Tax (q.v.) which is based on the share of the estate received by each beneficiary. Estate duty (or death duty) is simpler and more productive than inheritance tax because the former avoids the difficult task of determining the value of the share of each inheritor. Estate duty is usually levied at a progressive rate to reduce economic disparities.

Justification for Estate Duty: The institution of inheritance is a major contributory factor for inequalities of income and wealth and their perpetuation in modern societies. Estate taxation, if designed properly, can improve the distribution of economic power without much resistance.

Transfer of property has always been considered an appropriate base for taxation by governments, which not only protect privately-owned properties but also supervise their transfer from one generation to another. With the deceased's property subject to charge of estate duty, there is almost an assumption that there is a prior claim of the state over that of the legal heirs. Besides, the incidence of this levy is felt the least since inheritance is a mere bounty.

Estate duty can be avoided if property is transferred through gifts among living persons. To prevent such possibilities, estate duty is generally accompanied by a gift tax on the donor. Similarly, inheritance tax is associated with a gift tax on the donee. The basic philosophy underlying estate taxation is to curtail an individual's right to acquire property without his own efforts. However, estate taxation does not interfere with the right of a person to use his property during his lifetime.

Issues in Estate Duty: Although bearing a sound social philosophy (to promote a more equitable distribution of wealth) and being least objectionable on efficiency grounds, implementation of estate taxation bristles with difficult technical, social, and economic problems. An appropriate solution of these problems is necessary from equity angle.

1. To what extent does society desire to abridge a person's right to transfer property through bequest? The question pertains to exclusions, deductions, exemption limits, and rate progression. For example, if society wishes to impose a ceiling on such transfers, it may impose a 100 per cent duty on the value of the estate in excess of the ceiling limit.

2. Should the limits imposed on bequests apply irrespective of the relation between the recipient and the deceased? It would, of course, be unfair to treat the spouse and a distant relative of the deceased equally under the law of estate duty. In other words, tax treatment of estate should be lenient in case of close, and stricter in case of distant, family relationship with the deceased. For this purpose differential rates may be prescribed depending on the closeness of the family ties between the testator and the donee.

3. Should an individual's right to pass on wealth be curtailed more severely as successive generations become beneficiaries? According to Italian economist Eugenio Rignano, the level of applicable rates may rise as the property passes through successive bequests. The foregoing

issues are value-laden and therefore defy universally acceptable solutions. See also Quick Succession Relief.

Euro

This is the name of a new common currency of the European Union which is going to replace all other currencies of the member countries. It was introduced on 1.1.1999 and is likely to become fully operational by January 2002. Euro's birth is being hailed as a historic turning point in international finance and is arguably the greatest single step in the drive to create a united Europe from the ruins of World War II.

Some 50 billion coins and 13 billion notes will be needed to replace existing currency and they will not be ready until 2002. The euro zone grouping (Germany, France, Austria, Belgium, Finland, Ireland, Italy, Luxembourg, Netherlands, Portugal and Spain) will account for nearly a fifth of world economic output and trade and its significance was immediately apparent.

Economic and monetary union has been a recurring ambition of the European Union since the late 1960s because it promises both currency stability and a strong advance towards the integration of Europe. The transition to euro is likely to be smooth because the changeover is backed by solid legal guarantees and the financial markets are carefully preparing for the creation of the euro.

Euro is the single currency of participating countries from January 1, 1999. National currencies in these countries will continue to be legal tender until 2002, but only as sub-units of the euro. During the transitional phase between 1999 and 2002, use of the euro will neither be obligatory, nor prohibited. But the euro will be heavily used from the start.

Monetary policy and the financial markets will switch to the euro on that date. It will also be used by many large companies, especially those with substantial export business. Stability of euro is guaranteed by the fact that conditions laid down for its creation are strict and that it will be managed by an independent central bank.

Eurobanks

These are banks dealing in Eurocurrency/Eurodollar deposits or issuance of Eurobonds.

Eurodollar

It refers to dollar deposits owned by someone other than a resident of USA. The concept of Eurodollar came into existence in Europe during the late 1950s with the advent of currency convertibility. At that time, USA was losing dollars due to balance of payments deficit. These dollars were being deposited in European banks. Since dollar is the most acceptable currency, it moves from one country to another in search of higher interest rates. This movement of dollars has limited the effect of an independent monetary policy. For example, a country facing inflation may raise interest rate. However, this hike can attract more dollars leading to higher domestic money supply.

European Economic Community (EEC)

EEC was established by the Treaty of Rome signed on March 25, 1957, and which came into force in January 1958. EEC was preceded by the European Coal and Steel Community (ECSC), which became effective in July 1952 and created a common market in coal and steel for Belgium, France, Germany, Italy, Luxembourg and the Netherlands.

The Rome Treaty not only established EEC but also Euratom, providing for a common European Atomic Energy Community.

EEC quickly moved toward the accomplishment of its major goals: in December 1961, all quantitative restrictions on industrial goods traded among member countries were abolished; in July 1967, a common agricultural policy was enunciated; in July 1968, a common market was established that provided for the free movement of goods and labour and a common external tariff. In July 1967, ECSC, Euratom, and EEC institutions were merged into a single set of governing organisations, which has become known as the European Community.

The objective of EEC is to promote the harmonious development of economic activities, balanced expansion, increased stability, a rising standard of living, and closer relations among the member countries. Among the primary goals of EEC are the elimination of customs duties and quotas, establishment of a common tariff and commercial policy in contrast to other countries, free movement of persons, services, and capital, and establishment of a common policy pertaining to agriculture and transport.

In January 1973, Denmark, Italy, and the United Kingdom became associated with the EEC, and a system of free trade agreements in industrial commodities was negotiated with the members of the European Free Trade Association (EFTA). The European Monetary Agreement was instituted in March 1979, laying the foundation for increasing financial integration and a system of fixed but adjustable exchange rates, a common unit of account and the eventual formation of a European Monetary Fund. The first direct elections to the European Parliament were held in June 1979.

The Treaty of Rome established four central institutions for the governance of the EEC: the European Parliament, the Council of Ministers, the Commission, and the Court of Justice. Each of these institutions has, and continues to play, a unique role in the governance of the European community of nations.

European Monetary Union (EMU)

The aim of the Union is to restrict the fluctuations among participating currencies to a given maximum spread and to float them jointly against dollar. Also referred as European currency bond or *snake*. See also European Snake.

European Snake

It is a working agreement between various European states whereby they have agreed to keep their exchange rates in line with one another within close limits. The official name of this arrangement is European System of Narrower Exchange Rate Margins. It is called a *snake* because when exchange rates of member countries are plotted on a graph against a non-member currency, say dollar, they move together across the graph as a band of intertwined lines like snakes. See also European Monetary Union.

European Union (EU).

A 15-nation economic union in Western Europe comprising of Austria, Belgium, Britain, Denmark, Finland, France, Germany, Greece, Ireland, Italy, Luxembourg, the Netherlands, Portugal, Spain and Sweden.

Ex

In finance, ex means *without, not including.* In commerce, ex means *from*. Thus, ex warehouse means *sold from a warehouse, i.e.* buyer of the goods has to provide and pay for transport from the warehouse. Similarly, ex factory price means price from or at the factory, i.e. price before the inclusion of excise duty. Ex as a prefix means former, e.g. ex prime minister.

Ex Ante and Ex Post

According to Swedish economist Gunnar Myrdal (1898-1987), there is an important distinction between ex ante (prospective) and ex post (retrospective) methods of calculating economic quantities. Thus, ex ante demand is the quantity which buyers wish or intend to buy at the going price. It is contrasted with the ex post demand, i.e. quantity actually bought.

Excess Burden of Taxation

Excess burden (or dead-weight loss or efficiency cost) refers to the reduction in consumers' welfare over and above their loss of income as a result of tax payment. It arises due to changes in the relative prices of taxed and untaxed commodities in the post-tax period. Distortions in consumers' choices between goods, or producers' choices between factors, brought about by the imposition of taxes are burdensome to taxpayers without bringing any benefit to the government. Hence, they should be minimised. Economic efficiency is defined in terms of neutrality of taxation and aims at minimising or eliminating dead-weight loss.

When a tax is imposed, the spending power of a taxpayer is reduced. This is called the income effect of taxation and does not in itself result in economic inefficiency. However, when a tax affects relative prices, inducing individuals to substitute one commodity for another, it generates a substitution effect. which causes economic inefficiency by interfering with consumers' choices. More the distortion, the greater is the excess burden and vice versa.

Dead-weight loss is minimised when a set of differential *ad valorem* rates is imposed such as to reduce the production of all commodities in equal proportion. However, it is not easy to fix tax rates on different goods so that the demand for them is reduced proportionately. Since the (price) elasticity of demand for various goods is different, it would require different tax rates on these goods. In general, goods with relatively inelastic demand would have to be taxed at a higher rate than goods with relatively elastic demand. The practical problems of this approach limit its validity.

Excess Profit Tax

It is an additional tax on profits above a specified level which is defined as normal profit. Excess profit tax is usually imposed during emergencies such as a war. The purpose is to capture those additional profits which arise due to high government spending during wartime. The tax was imposed in Britain from 1939 to 1946 on all trades and businesses and was charged on the amount by which the profits exceeded the standard based on past profits.

Excess profit tax was levied in India in 1940. It was imposed on profits earned by businesses and professions during the period September 1, 1939 to March 31, 1946. A standard profit was calculated for each accounting year falling within the above years. Standard profit was approximately equated with the profits earned in normal times, i.e. in the pre-War years.

Companies started before 1936 had the following five options to choose from for determining standard profit: profits during 1935-36 or 1936-37 or average of the profits during 1935-36 and 1936-37 or 1936-37 and 1937-38 or 1937-38 and 1938-39. In the case of companies started after 1936, the capital standard was used, i.e. 8 per cent of the capital invested was considered the standard rate of profit. Excess profit tax was levied at the rate of 50 per cent on the excess over the standard profits earned between September 1, 1939 and March 31, 1941. For the period April 1, 1941 to March 31, 1946, the rate of excess profit tax was 66.6 per cent.

Exchange Control

It means control on the purchase and sale of foreign exchange at the official exchange rate by the central bank of a country. Regulation of foreign exchange transactions is generally done by a country facing balance of payments deficit in order to keep the foreign exchange reserves at appropriate level.

Exchange Position

It refers to the net result of a bank's sales and purchases of foreign exchange. If sales are more than purchases, it will show a minus balance. If purchases are more than sales, there will be a credit balance. If both are equal (nil balance) it is a square position.

Exchange Rate

It is the rate at which the currency of one country is converted into another currency. For example, Rs. 43 = 1 US $ is Indian rupee exchange rate for one US dollar.

Nominal Exchange Rate: It is the official parity for transactions as settled by a country's monetary authority.

Effective Exchange Rate: Apart from the nominal exchange rate, it includes all surcharges, tariffs, rebates and incentives on exports.

Price Level Deflated Exchange Rate (PLD-ER): Under it, the nominal exchange rate is deflated by the price index in relation to some base period.

Effective Exchange Rate (PLD-EER): It is the effective exchange rate deflated by the price index.

Purchasing Power Parity Adjusted Exchange Rate (PPPA-ER): It means the exchange rate (nominal or effective) is multiplied by the ratio of the foreign price level to domestic price level.

Real Effective Exchange Rate: In this case, the exchange rate is adjusted for inflation differentials between the country whose exchange rate is being measured and the country against which the exchange rate is calculated.

Forward and Spot Exchange Rates: Forward rate is the agreed rate of exchange at which a currency can be bought or sold today for delivery at some future date. Spot transactions are settled in two working days time. Forward exchange cover is a type of insurance that protects against movements in exchange rates and risks arising therefrom. As such, an exchange rate quoted for a forward date usually involves a premium or discount as compared with the spot rate.

Two-tier Exchange Rate: It means one exchange rate for commercial transactions and a separate exchange rate for financial transactions on current account.

Exchange Rationing

In the face of excess demand for foreign exchange over available supplies, the need is felt for its judicious allocation among individuals and firms which have to make payments for imports. Rationing is done according to the intensity and urgency of the need. It may also be used to force bilateral trade balancing, i.e. more is kept for imports from country A with which the country concerned has trade relations than for country B with which trade is not much.

Excise Duty

It is a tax on goods produced or manufactured within a country. It is collected from the producers of excisable goods.

Excise duty is levied either on *ad valorem* basis (i.e. as a percentage of the value of production) or on specific basis (i.e. as a stated amount per unit of weight, volume etc.) or on *ad valorem*-cum-specific basis.

Rules of Excise Taxation: The Indian Fiscal Commission, 1921-22, enunciated the following five golden rules of excise taxation which, with necessary modifications, seem to be relevant to this day.

1. Excise duties should ordinarily be confined to industries which are concentrated in large factories or small areas.

2. They may properly be imposed for the purpose of checking consumption of injurious articles, especially

luxuries coming under this category. Otherwise they should be imposed for revenue purpose only.

3. While permissible on commodities of general consumption, they should not press too heavily on poorer classes.

4. When an industry requires protection, any further necessary taxation on its products may, if the other conditions are fulfilled, take the form of excise duty *plus* an additional import duty. The latter should fully countervail the former and may be pitched at a higher price.

Exemptions

Exemptions (or exclusions) are those items which are explicitly and statutorily freed from the scope of a tax and therefore remain untaxed. They may be termed as non-taxable gross receipts. Several considerations weigh on a government to declare a host of receipts exempt, either fully or up to specified limits, from the scope of taxation.

Income tax laws of most countries describe incomes that are exempt from the purview of income tax, i.e. tax-free incomes. These exemptions serve various socio-economic objectives through the medium of tax policy. In developing countries, agricultural incomes are generally exempt from income tax owing to administrative difficulties of reaching out to widely dispersed small and marginal farmers who in most cases are illiterate. Incomes of charitable and religious trusts are generally exempt from taxes.

However, if the number of exemptions is very large, it will narrow the tax base besides making the law complex. See also Tax Holiday.

Exotic Currency **See Currency**

Expenditure Tax

It is a tax on personal expenditure. The early proponents of expenditure tax include such celebrities as Leviathan Hobbes, John Stuart Mill, and Irving Fisher. In 1955, Nicholas Kaldor in his book *An Expenditure Tax* argued vigorously in favour of expenditure as a measure of an individual's taxpaying capacity. In 1978, J.E. Meade Committee Report on *The Structure and Reform of Direct Taxation* also argued for the superiority of expenditure tax over income tax while analysing the possibilities and problems of expenditure tax in the United Kingdom. The list of opponents of expenditure tax is no less distinguished. It includes, among others, Richard Musgrave, Richard Goode, and Carl Shoup. These experts have expressed themselves against expenditure tax mainly on account of administrative and compliance problems.

The first argument in favour of expenditure tax rests on the ground that individuals should be taxed on what they take out from the national pool in terms of goods and services (consumption), rather than on what they contribute in terms of labour and capital services (income). This traditional argument has its origin in the following observation of Leviathan Hobbes, "What reason is there, that he which laboureth much, and sparing the fruits of his labour, consumeth little, should be more charged, than he that liveth idlely getteth little, and spendeth all he gets: Seeing the one hath no more protection from the Commonwealth than the other."

Two objections can be raised against Hobbes's reasoning. 1. The income of an individual does not arise only through his work and capital services. It is also received through capital gains, monopoly power, gifts in marriage or otherwise, lottery prizes, and more commonly through inheritance. Defined comprehensively, income does not always refer to the *contribution* one can be said to have made to total output. 2. There is no apparent justification to regard a tax on expenditure (actual consumption) as more equitable than a tax on income (potential consumption). J.A. Kay and M.A. King in their book *The British Tax System* have opined, "A one-legged unemployed man who manages to maintain a low level of consumption by begging is unlikely to be seen as just as suitable an object of taxation as a wealthy miser who chooses to spend very little and counts his money each night."

The second argument in favour of expenditure tax is its supposedly favourable effects on savings. Firstly, it encourages savings because the more one saves, the greater is the tax benefit. Secondly, it avoids *double taxation of savings* as is allegedly the case under a system of income tax. Income tax is imposed on income when it is first received, and then on interest earned when the same income is saved. As against this, expenditure tax impinges on savings only once, i.e. when they are spent. In brief, an expenditure tax tends to induce savings because the more one saves the greater is the tax benefit.

The foregoing argument implicitly assumes that savings are a virtue for a country. This is not necessarily so. Increasing the rate of savings is by no means a high priority objective in developed countries some of which, in fact, face dangers of excessive savings. Furthermore, an increase in the amount that people wish to save does not necessarily mean an increase in the amount that people wish to invest.

If at all savings are to be encouraged, it can be done by making special provisions in the tax laws. In fact, income tax laws in most countries accord favourable treatment to savings not only by exempting them from taxation but also income arising out of them. These provisions can be further strengthened in case more savings are desired.

The law of marginal propensity to save states that with increasing income the propensity to save also increases. It follows that the rich who save more will be the major beneficiaries of expenditure tax. This may promote concentration of wealth in a few hands, leading to undesirable social and economic consequences.

Similarly, the *double taxation of savings* argument is untenable because by no standards interest earned on savings can be regarded as savings. In all fairness, interest earned does increase the ability-to-pay of an individual.

The third argument in favour of expenditure tax is that problem of averaging is less severe under it than under income tax. In their work already quoted, J.A. Kay and M.A. King maintain, "Problems of averaging are likely to be less severe also, because whereas an individual has little control over the timing of receipts of windfall gains he can choose when to spend his resources. Moreover, it seems likely that individuals prefer to maintain a relatively stable pattern of expenditure over a run of years, and not to enjoy a burst of spending in one year followed by relative deprivation in succeeding years."

The above reasoning is not necessarily correct. While it is true that fortunes in a speculative business are subject to fluctuations, people are fairly certain about their receipts from salaries, interest income, property income, gains of profession, and profits of less adventurous business. Conversely, unexpected expenditure to deal with sickness, accidents, and natural calamities is more serious a problem particularly in countries lacking social security arrangements. A proper perception of the expenditure pattern of families requires an understanding of the social and religious values of societies. For example, in many traditional societies it is quite common to spend one's life time savings in celebrating marriages or performing religious rituals. The treatment of such lumpy expenditure will be a special problem in administering an expenditure tax. Its burden will be heavy in those years in which a family's social and religious commitments are high compared to their income. In other words, bursts in spending are more grievous than fluctuations in income.

Administrative Problems: How is the annual expenditure of an individual to be computed? Administratively, expenditure tax is the most dreaded tax for fiscal authorities. The nightmare is partly the result of the nomenclature of the tax which suggests, *prima facie*, as if administration will have to keep records of the details of each taxpayer's expenditure. The proponents of expenditure tax argue that operation of an expenditure tax does not require an exhaustive listing of every purchase made during the tax year. In its simplest form the assessment of expenditure tax requires the assessment of a taxpayer's income and his net savings during the year. Net savings are to be deducted from his income to arrive at his expenditure for the year.

Expenditure = Income - Savings + Dissavings

where

Savings = Expenditure on assets + Money lent out + Repayment of loans made

Dissavings = Sales of assets + Money borrowed + Repayments received

Apparently, in any assessment of expenditure, the calculation of income is a prerequisite involving all problems of income assessment under the income tax system. Definition of income for purposes of calculating expenditure tax has to be broader from the one used for income tax purposes. It will include exempt receipts, gifts received etc. Similarly, net wealth would also have to include certain assets often excluded under wealth tax. A taxpayer will be obliged to periodically report information concerning the value of assets added to and withdrawn from savings. This would require a taxpayer to submit a statement of all assets and liabilities as at the end of the financial year. This statement would then be compared with the comparable statement submitted at the close of the preceding year so that correctness of reported additions to and withdrawals from net wealth could be ascertained.

Yet another administrative problem relates to the consumption of consumer durables. It would involve all problems of measuring depreciation of enduring assets. Similarly, there are goods and services which are consumed jointly by family members and it will be a problem to allocate this collective consumption among different members of the family. In short, expenditure tax is the proverbial Pandora's Box containing various conceptual and administrative difficulties the fear of which has greatly reduced the practicability of this tax.

Expenditure Tax in Practice: Following the recommendations of British economist Nicholas Kaldor (1908-1986), a tax on personal expenditure was first imposed in India on April 1, 1958. The tax was introduced as an adjunct to the personal income tax as a part of a scheme to evolve a self-checking system of direct taxes in

India. Expenditure tax was withdrawn in 1962 on account of insignificant revenue yield and its failure to restrain ostentatious expenditure in order to promote savings. It was reintroduced in 1964 with the hope that the tax would help lessen inequalities of income and wealth. However, the tax was repealed again in 1966 on grounds of burden on administration and inconvenience to assessees.

Introduction of expenditure tax proved abortive in Ceylon (now Sri Lanka) also where it was imposed in 1959 but withdrawn in 1963. The unsuccessful experiments of India, and Sri Lanka have deterred other countries to impose expenditure tax.

It is noteworthy that Nicholas Kaldor's proposal for expenditure tax in Britain in the early 1950s was turned down by the Chancellor of the Exchequer who termed it *too radical.* Similarly, in USA when the tax was proposed by the Treasury in 1942 the reaction of the Congress was so hostile that the suggestion had to be withdrawn within a week.

Expense Account

It refers to allocation of money which a businessman is allowed to spend personally on travelling and entertaining clients in connection with his business.

Explicit Cost **See Cost**

Export Duty **See Customs Duty**

Export-led Growth

It is a situation when a developing country relies mainly on its export earnings to help stimulate its economic development.

Exports

Exports are, in the conduct of foreign trade, goods taken from one country into another country with the first country called the exporter, the second the importer.

Export Subsidies

These are provisions of financial assistance to exporters for encouraging them to export and for making their exports cheaper and competitive in the foreign market.

External Currency Convertibility See **Currency Convertibility**

External Dollar

It refers to US dollar assets or liabilities held by financial institutions outside USA. Variously called Euro-dollar, Asian dollar, offshore dollar etc., they are not subject to control by USA government.

F

Face Value

Face value (or par value or nominal value) is the value printed on a document such as a share certificate. The printed value need not represent the issue price, redemption price or current market price.

Factoral Terms of Trade **See Terms of Trade**

Factor Endowments

They refer to relative amounts of different factors of production that a country has.

Factor Intensity

It refers to relative proportion of a particular factor to other factor/factors required to produce a given amount of some commodity. For example, if 4 units of capital and 1 unit of labour are needed to produce one tonne of steel, it will be called a capital-intensive commodity.

Factor Intensity Reversal

It occurs when changes in factor price ratio lead to reversal in the use of factors in the production of a commodity. For example, textile production which is labour-intensive at a time due to low wage rate may turn capital-intensive when wage rate goes up and cheaper capital (machinery) becomes available.

Factor Price Equalisation Theorem

In a two country, two commodity, two factor situation with identical production functions and absence of complete specialisation, it can be shown that free trade will equalise the prices of traded goods in both the markets. Since the product prices are related directly to the factor prices, the latter will be equalised too. However, the assumptions of the theorem are too restrictive to bring a complete and absolute factor price equalisation.

Factors of Production

Basically, there are four factors of production: land, labour, capital and enterprise. Production becomes possible with the help of these factors of production.

Land: Land means all free gifts of nature including land as such, fertility of soil, sea, sunshine and rainfall. Land as a factor of production possesses the following characteristics: (a) it is fixed in supply, (b) it is immobile, (c) it is a passive factor of production, (d) it is heterogeneous. The reward for the services of land is called rent.

Labour: Labour refers to various types of physical and mental exertions of man. According to British classical economist Adam Smith (1723-1790), labour is the source of all wealth. It has the following characteristics: (a) labour is an active factor of production, (b) labour is mobile, (c) labour is perishable, (d) labour cannot be separated from the labourer, (e) efficiency of labour varies and (f) labour needs incentives to work.

Reward for the services of labour is called wages.

Capital: Capital refers to man-made machines, equipment, tools and implements which are used for further production of wealth. The reward for the services of capital is called interest.

Enterprise: Enterprise means bearing risks and uncertainties associated with business. He who bears these risks and uncertainties is called entrepreneur. He combines and organises other factors of production.

Reward for the services of an entrepreneur is called profit. Profit is a residual income after other factors of production have been paid. Unlike the rewards of other factors, profit cannot be determined in advance and it can be negative (loss) also.

Faked Invoicing

In order to take advantage of export subsidies, import entitlements etc., there is a tendency for over-invoicing of exports so that higher premiums can be earned. When these incentives are withdrawn, over-invoicing becomes less attractive and so exports are also shown to be less.

Similarly, if imports are on restricted category, there is a tendency to under-invoice them so that more volume of them could be had.

F.A.S.

Free Alongside Ship. It is a slight variation of F.O.B. valuation. It excludes cost of loading while F.O.B. includes it.

Federal Reserve System (FRS)

It refers to the system of twelve regional FRS banks in the USA which carry out the role of a central bank. The twelve banks are in Boston, New York, Philadelphia,

Cleveland, Richmond, Atlanta, Chicago, St. Louis, Minneapolis, Kansas City, Dallas and San Francisco.

Fee

Fee is charged by public authorities for providing certain services such as registration of marriages, births and deaths. Generally, the fee is charged equal to the cost of a service.

Feudalism **See Modes of Production**

Fiat Money **See Money**

Fiduciary Money **See Money**

Final and Intermediate Products

National income is the aggregate value of all final goods and services produced by a country, over a period of one year, for consumption and investment. To avoid double counting of goods, a distinction is made between intermediate and final goods.

If a product (commodity or service) is sold by one business unit to another for resale or for further production in the same year, it is called an intermediate product. Such goods are required mostly for use in production of other goods and services. For example, a bicycle is a final commodity but its parts like handle, tyres, frame and chain are intermediate goods. The demand for intermediate goods is known as *derived demand* because it is derived from the demand for final goods which satisfy consumers' wants. Similarly, goods lying with wholesalers and retailers for resale in the same year are also known as intermediatc goods.

If the product is sold not for resale or for further production, but for personal consumption then it is called final product. Final goods do not require further processing nor are they resold. The demand for these commodities is direct since they satisfy the wants of consumers directly. Bread, butter, residential buildings are examples of final goods.

The basis of distinction between final and intermediate goods is not the commodity itself but the use made of it. A building used for residential purpose is a final good but the same building becomes intermediate good when used as a factory.

Finance Bill

In India, budget of the Central Government contains proposals regarding both direct and indirect taxes. These proposals pertaining to the levy of new taxes, modifications of the existing tax structure or continuance of the existing rates of taxation for a further period are presented through the Finance Bill. The Finance Bill is presented to the Parliament on the same day as the Budget. Taxation proposals take effect the moment the Finance Bill is presented, indirect taxes immediately and direct taxes on a date specified in the Bill (normally the first day of the ensuing year, i.e. April 1). It is only after the Finance Bill is passed and becomes the Finance Act, does the collection of revenue get legislative authority.

Financial Intermediaries

Financial intermediaries are an integral part of a modern industrial economy. They are institutions which act as middlemen between the lenders and the borrowers. They specialise in the purchase and sale of financial assets. More specifically, they buy primary securities and sell secondary securities.

Financial intermediaries are classified into two main categories: (a) banks and (b) non-banking financial institutions like Unit Trust of India.

Financial intermediaries are beneficial both to lenders and borrowers. Lenders stand to gain because they can invest their funds at low risk and greater liquidity with financial institutions. The main advantage to borrowers is availability of adequate credit at reasonable rate of interest.

How are financial intermediaries able to benefit both lenders and borrowers and also to make profit for themselves in the process? The secret of their economic success lies in the economies of scale in asset management. They diversify their asset holdings in such a manner as to strike an optimum balance between security and profitability. For this purpose, the financial institutions employ professional managers and financial analysts who evaluate investment opportunities and take appropriate decisions. Because of the large volume of business, the establishment cost per unit of transaction is lower as compared to that of an individual investor.

Financial Market

It is a market in which financial assets of various kinds like shares, debentures and bills are dealt with. A financial market consists of (a) money market which deals in short-term credit and (b) capital market which provides medium-term and long-term credit.

Money Market: In a developing country like India money market is sub-divided into (a) organised market and (b) unorganised market. Commercial banks, co-operative banks and non-banking financial institutions comprise the organised sector of the money market. This market operates under the control, guidance and supervision of the central bank.

The unorganised money market predominates in rural areas and is composed of indigenous bankers and moneylenders. It is generally free from the monetary and credit controls of the central bank. It operates without a set of well-defined rules and regulations and is, therefore, exploitative in its dealings. The malpractices of moneylenders are well-known.

Capital Market: Like money market, the capital market is also divided into two sectors: (a) organised market comprising of development banks, share market and mutual funds and (b) unorganised market consisting of hire purchase companies, chit funds, finance companies etc. The unorganised sector of the capital market has limited importance.

Financial Reserves

Financial reserves of a country are a measure of economic strength used by international lenders and investors in judging risks. Hard currencies are usually in strong demand because they are backed by substantial reserves and general economic strength while soft currencies lack these attributes.

Financial reserves usually include gold, US dollars, other key currencies and special drawing rights (SDRs) issued by the IMF. In recent years, the official IMF policy has been to de-emphasise gold as too inflexible a reserve for dynamic global monetary and economic purposes, but the use of gold persists. SDRs are based on a basket of currencies and are made available to IMF members by allocation from time to time to provide additional liquidity for the international monetary system. SDRs, however, are restricted exclusively for government-to-government use.

Financial System

It refers to the whole gamut of institutional arrangements which help to mobilise financial surpluses of an economy and transfer them to areas of financial deficit. Financial system of a country rests on three pillars: (a) financial institutions or financial intermediaries, (b) financial markets and (c) financial assets.

Financial system is the linchpin of a modern industrial economy. It promotes savings by providing a wide variety of financial assets to the general public. Savings collected from the household sector are pooled together and allocated to various sectors of the economy for raising production level. If the allocation of credit is socially equitable, it will help in reducing interregional inequalities.

Financial Year

It is the year of account for financial purposes, often not coinciding with the calendar year. For example, in India the financial year (or fiscal year) runs from April 1 to March 31 of the following year. In USA, the fiscal year runs from July 1 to June 30 .

Fine

A fine is a compulsory payment without any *quid pro quo* to curb certain offence. It is different from a tax because the objective is not to get revenue for the government.

Firm

A firm is a unit which takes decisions regarding production and sale of commodities. A firm seeks profit by producing and selling commodities. More precisely, profit maximisation is the objective function of every firm. Profit (P) is the difference between revenue (R) received from the sale of output (Q) and the cost (C) of producing the output.

$$P = R - C$$

For determining the profit maximising output of a firm, it is necessary to understand the relationship between cost and output as well as revenue and output. The theories of cost and revenue are then combined to determine the most profitable output for a firm. However, before relating cost to output, it is necessary to know the relationship between output and input. Thus, the sequence of analysis becomes as follows:

1. How is output related to inputs (production function)?
2. How is cost related to output (cost function)?
3. How is revenue related to output (revenue function)?
4. Combination of cost and revenue functions to determine equilibrium of the firm, i.e. profit-maximising output.

It may be noted that cost conditions are common to all firms irrespective of the type of market in which they operate.

However, revenue conditions differ depending upon the market structure in which a firm operates. Perfect competition, monopoly, oligopoly and monopolistic competition (imperfect competition) are the important types of market in which firms generally operate.

Fiscal Capacity

It refers to the ability of an individual to pay taxes or the ability of a government to raise revenues.

Fiscal Conservatism

It maintains that governments seek to maximise their own utility functions rather than social welfare. This they do by spending as much as they can and by levying as few taxes as possible. Spending is attractive because some of it (salaries, allowances, expense accounts, and pensions of civil servants and legislators) is for the government's own consumption. Taxation is unpleasant as it angers the voters. Hence, many governments resort to large budget deficits. See also Deficit Financing.

Fiscal Deficit

Fiscal deficit is the difference between revenue receipts plus certain capital receipts (which are not borrowings and accrue finally to the government) *and* total expenditure including loans net of repayments. In other words, fiscal deficit means net borrowings of all kinds by a government. These borrowings are from (a) the public under various small saving schemes, (b) commercial banks and other financial institutions and (c) central bank. Fiscal deficit makes no distinction between one type of borrowing and the other although the implication of borrowings from central bank is different from borrowings from other sources.

Fiscal deficit = (Revenue receipts + Recoveries of loans + Other receipts) - Total expenditure.

or

Borrowings + Overall budgetary deficit

Fiscal Drag

In a period of inflation, the value of money decreases. Therefore, the value of exemptions, deductions, and allowances allowed in the computation of income and tax liability becomes less in real terms. The brackets of taxable income chargeable at progressive rates also shrink in real terms. Taxpayers are pushed into higher income bands (and therefore higher rates) because of increasing money income which in real terms may remain the same. The higher rate of income tax may lead to reduction in real income owing to this fiscal drag.

Fiscal Federalism

A federal set up creates a multiple polity based on divided functions and powers among central, state and local governments. Fiscal federalism deals with financial arrangements and their working in a federal polity.

Federal system of government is a mixed blessing. It has the advantage of economic integration which promotes industrial and defence capabilities of a nation. Simultaneously, decentralised decision-making meets the politico-economic aspirations of the people at the sub-national level. Furthermore, decentralisation of governmental functions allows better matching of supplies of public goods to local needs and hence increases social welfare. However, a country cannot reap fully the economies of scale if provision for public goods is decentralised.

Fiscal Marksmanship

It refers to the degree of accuracy of budgetary forecasts. Extensive estimates of revenue and expenditure are set forth in the budget of a government for the ensuing financial year.

The *actuals* or *accounts* of the revenue and expenditure become available after the expiry of the financial year under consideration. Perfectly accurate estimates of revenue, and expenditure are never possible and therefore some divergence is always there between the *budget estimates* and the *actuals*.

The degree of deviation between the two indicates the skill and competence of budget-makers. Excessive deviation reveals the poor fiscal predictability (or marksmanship) of the experts.

The nature and degree of divergence between *budget estimates* and *actuals* is of considerable importance in the context of resource mobilisation, economic planning, financial stability, and tax burden. This divergence has two aspects:

(a) over-estimation and

(b) under-estimation.

Over-estimation of revenue ends up with shortages of funds, leading to curtailment or even abandonment of certain developmental projects. In case the public expenditure is inelastic, over-estimation of revenue will necessitate larger deficit financing. Furthermore, over-estimation of tax revenue may slacken governmental efforts to mobilise resources through other sources.

Conversely, under-estimation of tax revenue means unwarranted tax doses. Apart from antagonising the public, unexpected resources in the hands of public authorities are likely to be wasted on unproductive projects formulated at short notice. Under-estimation of revenue may induce a government to resort to public borrowings thereby increasing the liabilities of the public exchequer unnecessarily.

$$\text{Error in budget estimates} = \frac{(\text{Actual - Budget})}{\text{Budget}} \times 100$$

Positive errors depict under-estimation and negative errors over-estimation.

The Public Accounts Committee of the Indian Parliament in its 27th Report expressed the view that variations in budget versus actual figures of more than 4 per cent should be a matter of concern. If this figure is accepted as the reasonable margin of error, then deviations of more than 4 per cent between *actuals* and the *budget estimates* of revenue and expenditure can be said to indicate poor fiscal marksmanship of the budget experts.

Fiscal Monopolies

These are non-financial public enterprises exercising monopoly in the production and/or distribution of such commodities as tobacco, alcoholic beverages, and salt. Using the monopoly power, revenues are raised for the government which may otherwise be gathered through taxes if such commodities are produced/distributed by private units.

Fiscal Policy

It refers to the use of a government's taxation and expenditure policies to influence the level of economic activities at the macroeconomic level. According to Ursula Hicks (1896-1985), "Fiscal Policy is concerned with the manner in which all the different elements of public finance, while still primarily concerned with carrying out their own duties (as the first duty of a tax is to raise revenue), may collectively be geared to forward the aims of economic policy." Export-import duties, subsidies etc. are important instruments of fiscal policy on the external front.

Fiscal Year **See Financial Year**

Fixed Asset **See Asset**

Fixed Cost **See Cost of Production**

Fixed Exchange Rate System

It is a system under which the value of a currency is tied by the central bank to important currencies like dollar, pound or gold or SDRs. Only marginal fluctuations are permitted.

Flat Rate

Fixed rate of tax regardless of the amount of income.

Floating Debt **See Ways and Means Advances**

Floating Exchange Rate System

It is a system in which the prices of various currencies relative to each other are set by the forces of demand and supply in the market without any intervention by the government.

Flows **See Stocks and Flows**

Flying Geese Pattern of Development **See Product Cycle**

F.O.B.

Abbreviation for free on board. It is a price quotation indicating that the seller is responsible for all costs of shipment of goods, including responsibility for damage or loss, up to a certain named point. For example, F.O.B. buyer's plant means the seller is responsible for the cost of the goods and their transportation and arrival in good condition at the buyer's plant.

Foreign Aid

There is no consensus on what constitutes foreign aid. Economists usually consider aid as international flow of resources in the form of public development assistance. If this assistance is from individual national governments, it is called *bilateral aid*. If it is from international donor agencies like UNO and other global bodies, regional development banks and aid consortia, it is called *multilateral aid*.

Thus, foreign aid is any international transfer made on concessional terms (rather than at market/commercial terms) for promoting economic development. International financial transfers can take two forms: (a) grants and (b) loans. Grants are unilateral transfers which are not to be repaid. Loans carry relatively lower rate of interest and longer period of repayment. Foreign aid may take a variety of physical forms such as capital goods, commodities (especially food), technical assistance and military equipment. Normally, military aid is not considered as part of foreign aid.

Many believe that foreign aid from rich countries is indispensable for the development of less developed countries (LDCs). If LDCs wish to emerge from poverty, they must save and invest. Foreign aid can help them fill the gap between low level of domestic savings and desired level of investment. Foreign aid may bring with it managerial skills and technical know-how. This will help LDCs to discard their outdated methods of production. Better technology is the key to increased productivity. It is also argued that aid is an international redistributive mechanism. The widening gap between developed and underdeveloped countries can be reduced through foreign aid. It is the moral duty of the rich nations to help the starving people of Africa and Asia. The present poverty of LDCs is partly attributed to their economic exploitation by the developed countries of Europe and America.

Adverse repercussions of foreign aid are also noteworthy. Opponents believe that foreign aid is neither a necessary nor a sufficient condition for emerging from poverty. There is considerably more to development than just injections of aid. Economic achievement depends on people's own faculties, motivations, ways of life, institutions and the policies of their rulers.

Giving aid reinforces the fatalist attitudes of LDC governments. It also creates feeling of inferiority among the people of recipient country. Aid impairs the spirit of competitiveness among LDCs. If aid is in the form of loans, it adds to the burden of debt which is already massive in amount in the case of LDCs. Repayment of loans leads to foreign exchange outflows from LDCs, accentuating their balance of payment difficulties.

Almost invariably, aid is available to LDCs with restrictions, particularly regarding its use. The tying of aid may take the following forms: (a) *Source tying or procurement tying:* It specifies where the recipient can spend aid. The spending restrictions usually take the form of tying aid to purchases in the donor country. This reduces the real worth of aid because it prevents recipients from 'shopping around the world to find exactly the goods they want in the cheapest markets. The recipient country must buy imports in the donor country and they are to be transported in ships of donor country. (b) *Use-tying:* Aid is tied to specific projects which may not be in line with the development goals of LDCs. (c) *Double-tying:* More often than not, both restrictions operate together, leading to double tying. This has been extremely expensive for LDCs. The prices from tied sources are much higher than the international prices.

Aid-tying is justified by the donors as necessary for overcoming their balance of payment deficits. However, source-tying is adopted by not only balance of payment deficit countries (e.g. USA) but also by surplus countries (e.g. Japan and Germany).

Source-tying is also governed by the desire of donors to support their industries with excess capacity or to get rid of their surplus stocks of commodities. Thus, aid with strings is less useful for LDCs than it may appear overtly. In fact, tied-aid creates more jobs and leads to the establishment and expansion of more industries in the donor than in the donee country.

Foreign Direct Investment

Investment in one country by individuals and organisations from another is an important aspect of international economics. Investment may be for portfolio (i.e. in the form of securities) or direct capital (i.e. productive facilities).

Foreign Direct Investment (FDI) is the outcome of the mutual interests of multinational firms and host countries. According to the International Monetary Fund, FDI is defined as "investment that is made to acquire a lasting interest in an enterprise operating in an economy other than that of the investor. The investor's purpose being to have an effective voice in the management of the enterprise." [11]. It should not be confused with portfolio investment, which does not seek management control, but is motivated by profit. Portfolio investment occurs when individual investors invest, mostly through stockbrokers, in stocks of foreign companies in foreign land in search of profit opportunities.

The wave of liberalisation and globalisation sweeping across the world has opened many national markets for international business. Global private investment, in most part, is now made by transnational corporations (TNCs) also referred to as multinational corporations (MNCs). Clearly, these transnational organisations play a major role in world trade and investments because of their demonstrated management skills, technology, financial resources, and related advantages.

Dilemma is faced by developing nations in formulating policies covering investments by foreigners. They usually have an urgent need for foreign investment assistance, but domestic political considerations often dictate severe tax and other laws, including nationalisation laws, which discourage new foreign investment. Many developing nations have been successful, however, in providing attractive tax and other incentives to foreign investors for sufficient time periods to ensure a satisfactory return on the original investment.

Advantages: Private foreign investment, mostly by multinational corporations, is an important form of international flow of financial resources. Foreign investment takes place for private gain but it has the following potential benefits for less developed countries (LDCs): (a) foreign investment can fill the gap between desired investment and locally mobilised savings, (b) it can fill the gap between desired foreign exchange requirements and those derived from net export earnings, (c) foreign investment can supply a package of needed resources such as management experience, entrepreneurial abilities, organisational and technological skills, (d) foreign investment brings with it technological knowledge while transferring machinery and equipment to LDCs, (e) foreign investment can create employment in the modern sectors of LDCs, (f) it can benefit consumers in LDCs through lower prices/improved quality of goods and through new products, (g) foreign investment can stimulate domestic investment through forward and backward linkages. For example, output of a foreign firm can be an input of domestic industries. Similarly output of the domestic industries can be inputs for the foreign firms. If this is so, foreign firms create demand for industries producing goods purchased by them.

Disadvantages: Foreign private investment is not an unmixed blessing. Governments of LDCs have to be very careful while deciding the magnitude, pattern and conditions of private foreign investment. The adverse implications of foreign investment are the following : (a) when foreign investment is competitive with home investment, the profits in domestic industries fall, leading to fall in domestic savings, (b) contribution of foreign firms to public revenue through corporate taxes is considerably less because of liberal tax concessions, excessive investment allowances, disguised public subsidies and tariff protection provided by the host government, (c) foreign firms reinforce dualistic socio-economic structure and increase income inequalities. They create a small number of highly paid modern sector executives. They divert resources away from priority sectors to the manufacture of sophisticated products for the consumption of local elites. As they are located in urban areas, they create imbalance between rural and urban opportunities, accelerating flow of rural population to urban areas, (d) foreign firms stimulate inappropriate consumption patterns through excessive advertising and monopolistic/oligopolistic market power. The products made by multinationals for the domestic markets behind tariff walls are not necessarily low in price and high in quality. Their technology is generally capital-intensive which does not suit the needs of a labour-surplus economy, (e) foreign firms are able to extract sizeable economic and political concessions from competing governments of LDCs. These concessions may take the form of excessive protection, tax rebates and investment allowances. Consequently, private profits of these companies may exceed social benefits, (f) foreign firms try to avoid local taxes by artificially inflating the price they pay for intermediate products purchased from overseas affiliates so as to lower their stated local profits. This is known as *transfer pricing* and host governments have no control over this. They can also avoid the effects of domestic monetary policy because of easy access to foreign capital markets and their internal resources, (g) continual outflow of profits is too large in many cases, putting pressure on foreign exchange reserves. Foreign investors are very particular about profit repatriation facilities, (h) foreign firms may influence political decisions in LDCs. In view of their large size and power, national sovereignty and control over economic policy may be jeopardised. In extreme cases, they (foreign firms) may bribe public officials at the highest levels. Similarly, they may contribute to *friendly* political parties and subvert the political process of the host country.

Determinants of FDI: To understand the scale and direction of FDI flows, it is necessary to identify their major determinants. Factors influencing the destination of investment, i.e. the host-country determinants are examined below.

Size of the Market: Large countries provide substantial markets where the consumer demand for certain goods has been largely unfilled to date. This potential has been a draw for many of the initial foreign-owned operations in these countries. This explains the massive FDI flows which the large size of China's market has attracted since early 1980s. In many cases, the establishment of a low cost marketing operation represents the first step by a multinational into the market of the country. This establishes a presence in the market and provides important insights into the ways of doing business and possible opportunities in the country.

Uncertainty: In many countries, the institutions of government are still evolving and there are unsettled political questions. Companies are unwilling to contribute large amounts of capital into an environment where some of the basic political questions have not yet been resolved.

Macroeconomic Environment: Instability in the level of prices and the exchange rate makes business planning difficult and increases the level of uncertainty. This increases the perceived risk of making investments and so adversely affects the inflow of FDI.

Legal and Regulatory Framework: The transition towards a market economy entails the establishment of a legal and regulatory framework that is compatible with private sector activities and the operation of foreign-owned companies. The areas of importance in this field include protection of property rights, ability to repatriate profits, and a free market for currency exchange. It is important that these rules and their related administrative procedures are transparent and easily comprehensible.

Access to Basic Inputs: FDI can be attracted by a country through the easy availability of factors of production. Many developing countries have large reserves of skilled and semi-skilled workers that are available for employment at wages significantly lower than in developed countries. This provides an opportunity for foreign firms to make investments in these countries to cater to the export market. Availability of natural resources such as oil and gas, minerals and forestry products also determine the extent of FDI.

Foreign Exchange

Currencies of all other (foreign) countries against which the native currency can be exchanged.

Foreign Exchange Market

A market where any country's currency can be bought/sold for another country's currency. It does not refer to any geographical market.

Foreign Tax Credit See Double Taxation

Foreign Trade

Foreign trade is an important element of world economy. The importance of foreign trade differs from country to country. Normally, external trade is less important for countries having a wide geographical area and possessing a great variety of natural resources. Contrarily, the dependence on foreign trade is high for smaller countries endowed with less variety of resources.

Trade takes place because the facilities for the production of various goods are unequally distributed over the world. These facilities include (a) mineral deposits (b) soil and climatic conditions, (c) labour skills etc. Based on these differences in factor endowments, different regions of the world and different regions within a country specialise in the production of goods for which they are best suited.

In fact, the basis (or reason) for international trade is the same as for trade within a country viz. geographical specialisation. In other words, both international trade and inter-regional trade have their root in territorial specialisation. As Swedish economist Bertil Ohlin observed: "International trade is but a special case of inter-local or inter-regional trade."

Why should then one study international trade separately? The study of international trade as a separate subject from inter-regional trade is necessitated because the former poses certain peculiar problems. These are: (1) Exchange rate determination because of different currencies involved in international transactions. (2) The balance of payments problem. (3) Barriers to international trade in the form of tariffs (duties) and quotas.

Foreign Trade Accelerator

Charles Kindleberger showed how a rise in exports accelerates import surplus and a fall in exports accelerates export surplus. This principle works as follows: Rise in exports leads to an increase in national income and through that a rise in consumption expenditure and investment.

Higher investment leads to more capacity creation in domestic and export industries which ultimately leads to a higher level of imports. This principle works in reverse as well.

Foreign Trade Multiplier

In an open economy, apart from domestic investment, export earnings can also lead to a rise in national income which can be a multiple of initial earnings. The rise depends on the level of marginal propensity to consume, or in reverse on the levels of marginal propensities to save and import. Thus, foreign trade multiplier is a number which when multiplied with the initial rise in export earnings can tell us how much national income has increased due to exports.

Foreign Travel Tax

It is a tax on the price of ticket for air travel to other countries. It is a kind of levy on luxury spending.

Forfait Method

It is an assessment procedure used mainly with respect to small commercial and industrial units. The French forfait system is a typical example of this assessment technique. It has the following ingredients: 1. The taxable profit of a given business unit is agreed upon mutually between the tax authorities and the assessee. 2. The assessment remains valid for a limited number of years. 3. The taxpayer is required to submit a set of simple facts to the authorities, namely the amount of his purchases and sales, the value of his inventory, the number of employees and wages paid. Such obligations are less demanding than those facing taxpayers who are assessed directly on their actual income and must produce comprehensive accounts of their transactions. See also Presumptive Tax.

Forward and Spot Markets

Forward (or future) market relates to dealings in promises to buy/ sell goods, foreign exchange and securities at a fixed price at a future date. It is contrasted with spot (or cash) market which deals with prices for immediate delivery.

Forward Exchange Rate See Exchange Rate

Franked Income

Franked income (dividend etc.) means income free of a further charge because it has already suffered a tax.

Free Port

Free port or a free trade zone allows goods to be temporarily imported and held within the port area without paying duty, provided they are re-exported later. The goods may be stored, processed, and/or repackaged in this area, and then either imported in the normal way by paying customs duty or re-exported without paying tariff. Thus, Singapore is a free port and Kandla is a free trade zone.

Free Rider

A free rider is a person who receives benefits of a government service without paying for it.

Free Trade

It refers to absence of any form of government interference with the free flow of international trade.

Free Trade Area (FTA)

It comprises a group of partner countries which abolish all tariff barriers among themselves but continue to keep their individual tariff rates for other countries who are not members of FTA. It differs from a Customs Union (q.v.) in that each country may retain its own tariffs against other countries, rather than agreeing on a common uniform tariff between the free trade area members and the rest of the world.

Free Trade Zone See Free Port

Frequency Distribution

It is an important method to organise and summarise statistical data. Frequency is the number of times a particular value appears in a set of observations. The distribution of observations over the several values is called frequency distribution. In other words, the various items in a series are classified into groups and the number of items falling into each group is stated.

Full Dividend Imputation System See Corporate Income tax

Full Integration System See Corporate Income tax

Functional Finance

A term attributed to Abba Lerner, it emphasises the study of fiscal policy (taxation and spending) in terms of results rather than the traditional doctrine about what is appropriate or inappropriate.

Functional Relations

Economic analysis deals mainly with the behaviour of measurable quantities (such as money supply, prices, exports, budget deficit) and the relations among two or more of these quantities. The idea that there is a relationship between money supply (M) and prices (P) can be expressed as P = f (M) which is read *P is a function of M*. A function provides us with a rule for getting the value of one variable given the value of the other.

Future Trading

It refers to commodity or currency trading done on contract for future delivery. The purpose is to insure against risks of price changes, exchange rate changes etc. or to make a profit by speculating on the price trends.

G

Galloping Inflation See Hyperinflation

General Agreement on Tariffs and Trade (GATT)

GATT was technically an agreement, rather than an organisation, among various countries called contracting parties with a secretariat at Geneva. It had three main objectives: (a) to establish standards for the non-discriminatory commercial policies of the contracting parties, (b) to settle trade disputes and encourage mutual consultation between nations and (c) to discourage non-tariff barriers and sponsor tariff reductions through a series of multilateral negotiations and rounds. There were seven major tariff-cutting rounds, more important among them being Kennedy Round, Tokyo Round and the Uruguay Round.

GATT was turned into a new organisation named World Trade Organisation (WTO) on January 1, 1996.

General Equilibrium See Partial Equilibrium and General Equilibrium

Generalised System of Preferences (GSP)

These were negotiated under UNCTAD and based on the principle of removing tariff barriers for developing countries on a non-reciprocal basis. GSP mainly applies on designated manufactures and semi-manufactures with some exceptions for primary commodities. Since its origin in 1976, USA has extended GSP programme of duty free treatment to about 3000 items covering 140 developing countries.

Geneva Group

It is a group of important world coffee producers, viz. Brazil, Colombia, Portugal and Ivory Coast (with their share in world coffee output at 85 per cent). It broke off from International Coffee Organisation in 1972 to achieve an upward trend in coffee prices, set their own quotas and establish a buffer stock.

German Reparations

It refers to large amount of war damages claimed after World War I by Belgium, England, France and Italy from Germany. In a settlement in London in 1921, it was decided that Germany would pay reparations to the Allies equivalent to 132 billion gold marks over a twenty year period. This huge transfer of funds led to a thinking of what came to be known in literature as *transfer problem*. Firstly, it meant creating an export surplus equal to this amount. Then it meant converting payer's money (mark) into receiving countries' currency such as lira, franc, pound etc. This transfer was likely to affect terms of trade as well. From many angles, this transfer was not mere a money transfer but a real transfer as well.

Giffen Goods

These are commodities of relatively low quality which form significant part of the diet of poor people as, for example, wheat, potatoes and mustard oil. The demand for these commodities is sometimes observed to decrease with decrease in their prices and vice versa. Since this situation is contrary to the law of demand, it is also known as Giffen's paradox named after Robert Giffen (1837-1910) who first pointed it out. The explanation lies in the fact that a fall in the price of say wheat causes a rise in the real income of the consumers. After paying for wheat, the consumers are left with more to spend on superior consumption items (e.g. rice). Switch over to rice reduces the demand for wheat. See also Demand Theory.

Gift Tax

It is imposed on the aggregate value of gifts made by a person (donor) during the year. A gift is defined as a transfer by one person to another of any existing movable or immovable property made voluntarily and without consideration in money or money's worth. In other words, before a transfer of property becomes liable to gift tax, the following conditions must be satisfied: (a) the transfer must be voluntary, (b) the transfer must be of existing property and (c) the transfer must be without consideration in money or money's worth.

Gifts from one person to another provide a convenient device to avoid or reduce liability under income tax, wealth tax and estate duty. The objective of gift tax is to ensure that transfers of wealth which are effected during the lifetime of a person bear tax liability similar to the levy of estate duty on property passing on the death of a person. Thus, gift tax is used as a supplement to estate and inheritance taxes which are sought to be avoided by giving away property before death.

To compute gift tax liability, tax authorities have to find out the value of all the gifts made during the relevant fiscal year. There is no difficulty in the valuation of gifts so far as cash gifts are concerned. Problems of valuation arise in the case of gifts other than cash. In such cases, the value is taken to mean the amount which the property would fetch if sold in the open market on the date on which the gift was made.

Gilt-edged Securities

These are government securities free of risk of default.

Globalisation

Globalisation implies widening and deepening integration with the *globe*, i.e. with people and processes abroad. Further, at the end of the integrative effort there must lie some concrete benefits for the country, for otherwise the globalisation being attempted would not be worth the effort.

The trend towards the evolution of a global society is generally thought of in economic terms and in terms of the consequences of the revolution in communication technologies. There is undoubtedly much greater economic integration among the nations of the world today.

Globalisation is widely seen as the most important factor that could influence economies of nations the world over in the new millennium. The rapid advancement in information technology and communications has made it not just possible but absolutely essential for industry the world over to adapt or fall by the wayside.

The 1990s witnessed a paradigm shift towards market oriented economic policies and a careful dismantling of obstacles in its wake. This has helped the smaller, emerging economies gain access to world markets, emergent technologies and collaborations. This has also given them a window to the developed world and helped them understand the significant role of globalisation as an instrument, which could be utilised not just to achieve economic efficiency, but also eradicate poverty.

Globalisation has also resulted in the creation of a new business framework. More changes can be expected in the business scenario specifically in terms of openness, adaptiveness and responsiveness.

The most important aspects of economic globalisation are: (i) the breaking down of national barriers; (ii) the international spread of trade, financial and production activities, and (iii) the growing power of transnational corporations and international financial institutions in these processes. While economic globalisation is a very uneven process, with increased trade and investment being focused in a few countries, almost all countries are greatly affected by this process.

A major feature of globalisation is the growing concentration and monopolisation of economic resources and power by transnational corporations and by global financial firms and funds. This process has been termed transnationalisation, in which fewer and fewer transnational corporations are gaining a large and rapidly increasing proportion of world economic resources, production and market shares. Where a multinational company used to dominate the market of a single product, a big transnational company now typically produces or trades in an increasing multitude of products, services and sectors. Through mergers and acquisitions, fewer and fewer of these TNCs now control a larger and larger share of the global market, whether in commodities, manufactures or services.

A unique feature of the current globalisation process is the globalisation of national policies and policy-making mechanism. National policies (including economic, social, cultural and technological areas) that until recently were determined by the States and people within a country have increasingly come under the influence of international agencies and processes or by big private corporations and economic/ financial players. This has led to the narrowed ability of governments and people to make choices from options in economic, social and cultural policies.

Most developing countries have seen their independent policy-making mechanism capacity eroded, and have to adopt policies influenced by other entities, which may on balance be detrimental to the countries concerned. The developed countries, where the major economic players reside, and which also control the processes and policies of international economic agencies, are better able to maintain control over their own national policies as well as determine the policies and practices of international institutions and the global system. However, it is also true that the large corporations have taken over a large part of decision-making even in the developed countries, at the expense of the power of the State or political and social leaders.

But at the end of the day, one has to understand and accept that globalisation is the stratagem for the new millennium. Every country, developed and developing, has to accept this and formulate their economies around it. The issue that concerns developing countries is how one can ensure greater participation of the weaker economies in the global process and what needs to be done to ensure that the course of globalisation benefits more people in more countries.

The uneven and unequal nature of the present globalisation is manifested in the fast growing gap between the world's rich and poor people and between developed and developing countries; and by the large differences among nations in the distribution of gains and losses.

This imbalance leads to polarisation between countries and groups that gain, and the many countries and groups in society that lose out or are marginalised. Globalisation, polarisation, wealth concentration and marginalisation are therefore linked through the same process. In this process, investment resources, growth and modern technology are focused on a few countries, mainly in North America, Europe, Japan and a few East Asian countries. A majority of developing countries are excluded from the process, or are participating in it in marginal ways.

Although the developed world is in a dominant position and has been prepared to use this to further their control of the global economy, the developing countries have not done well in organising themselves to co-ordinate on substantial policy and negotiating positions. The developed countries, on the other hand, are well organised within their own countries, with well staffed departments dealing with international trade and finance, and with university academics and private and quasi government think tanks helping to obtain information and map policies and strategies. They also have well-organised associations and lobbies associated with their corporations and financial institutions, which have great influence over the government departments.

Globalisation is an irreversible trend and developing economies are also inevitably involved in the process. One should therefore, carefully consider how to restructure the world trading system to accommodate developing economies, by enabling them to benefit from globalisation while minimising external shocks. The WTO should work more effectively, through an enlargement of waiver clauses which recognise the weaker position of developing countries.

The socio-economically disadvantaged are yet to benefit from reform policies. The challenge to overcome the scourge of poverty remains a daunting task. The support of the poor for reforms, and their involvement in the development process can be achieved only if they start benefiting from the policies. It is necessary to ensure that the poor and the deprived have an even greater stake in economic reforms than at present for mobilising their enthusiastic participation in the development process. Economic reforms must be guided by compassion and distributive justice. Improvement of living conditions of the poorest and the weakest sections of society should be high priority areas in the first decade of the new millennium.

On the positive side, globalisation has compelled developing countries to improve overall economic management, and make their economies efficient. To get a share of global capital and technology, developing countries have to upgrade their social and economic institutions through administrative, legislative and legal reforms. The quality of governance has to improve to encourage productivity and efficiency. Political stability has to be established. If we were to draw lessons from the East Asian countries, we would get several valuable insights: (i) developing human capital is a basic pre-requisite. Successful globalisation and the knowledge economy require educated, healthy and skilled people; (ii) it is necessary to build up domestic savings and put it to productive use; (iii) sound economic management and macro-economic balances are necessary. Large fiscal deficit is a serious obstacle to globalisation; (iv) good governance at the national and sub-national level builds confidence among investors; (v) transparency has to be established in the functioning of both government and business units; (vi) free and open market economies require effective regulatory authorities, as government's role changes from control and regulation to governance and facilitation; (vii) modernised capital markets with effective regulatory authorities to impart confidence to investors by maintaining stability and regulating speculative forces.

Despite such distortions and aberrations, globalisation is a reality. Developments in information and communication technologies will unify markets and people, cutting across barriers of space and time.

Global Quota

It specifies total amount of a commodity which can enter into a country during a certain time period.

Global, Schedular and Dualistic Patterns of Taxation

A taxpayer may receive income from various sources. Are the different sources of income to be treated alike for applying a set of tax rates? If yes, the system will be called *global* in nature. In other words, the global principle of taxation does not distinguish between different sources of income. Income from all sources is pooled for the purpose of applying tax rates.

However, if various sources of income are subject to a series of separate taxes, the system is called *schedular* in character. If the system combines the features of both *global* and *schedular* patterns, it becomes *dualistic* or *composite* in nature. The superiority or suitability of a pattern depends on the nature of an economy (developed or underdeveloped), objectives of tax policy being pursued in a country, and the efficiency of the tax administration.

Gold Exchange Standard

It refers to a system which emerged after World War II featuring a fixed exchange rate policy defined in terms of gold. The rate of exchange was allowed to fluctuate within a narrow range around its official parity. This system was a mixture of gold exchange and reserve currency standard.

Gold Export Point

Under gold standard, it is an indicator of exchange rate beyond which gold of a country starts moving out. For example, when a USA buyer of pound sterling wanted to buy it he had to pay its price in the exchange market (mint parity rate) plus the cost of shipment of gold from USA to UK. For example, if the mint parity was \$ 2.50 for each pound and the cost of shipment was equal to 1 per cent of \$ 2.50, he had to pay a price of \$ 2.525 per pound sterling.

Thus, the USA buyer had an option of buying pound in New York itself at \$ 2.525 per pound. There was no point in exporting gold to London to buy pound which would cost the same. It was only when the market price in New York exceeded this price (mint parity plus cost of transportation) that gold would actually be exported to London to buy pound. Therefore, this price was the maximum which could be charged for each pound and it set the gold export point.

Gold Standard

This system operated during 1870 to 1914 and then during 1925 to 1931. It provided for almost fixed rates of exchange. Under this, all national governments were committed to buy and sell a specified amount of gold for a specified amount of their currency. Thus, if all countries did alike, the rate of exchange between them could be determined by the ratio of the gold parities.

For example, if USA agreed to buy and sell one fine ounce of gold for $ 35 and UK also agreed to buy and sell one fine ounce of gold for £14, then the exchange rate was settled at $ 35 = £ 14 or $ 2.50 = £ 1. This rate was called *mint parity*.

This rate of exchange could be changed by a country only by the price of gold in terms of its own currency. If USA wanted to change the price of dollar to $ 3 = £ 1, then it had to raise the price of gold to $ 42 per ounce.

Prior to 1914, gold standard was a type of monetary system with the following characteristics: the national monetary unit was defined in terms of a given quantity of gold; the central bank or treasury stood ready to buy and sell gold at the resulting fixed price in terms of the national currency; gold was freely coined and gold coin formed a significant part of the circulating medium; and gold could be freely exported and imported. The exchange rate between any two countries adhering to such arrangements was determined by the gold content of their respective monetary units and could vary from this parity only within a narrow band (the gold points) reflecting the cost of shipping gold from one country to the other. Private arbitrage shipments of gold, which became profitable when either of these limits was reached, prevented the band from being breached.

The objective of economic policy under the pre-1914 gold standard was to maintain the redeemability (convertibility) of the national currency directly or indirectly into gold at the legal parity, i.e. to keep exchange rates fixed against other gold standard currencies. From about 1880 to 1914 exchange rates among gold standard countries remained fixed without support of payments or import controls, with virtually no countries being forced off the gold standard once adopted.

During World War I most countries suspended the redeemability of their currencies into gold, withdrew gold coins from circulation, and concentrated gold holdings in official reserves. The currencies of most belligerent countries did not, however, depreciate by much in terms of gold and the dollar because of official pegging operations supported by gold sales, foreign borrowing, liquidation of assets abroad, and imposition of some import and exchange controls. At the end of the war, USA was virtually the only country on a full gold standard.

After the war, governments were eager to return to the gold standard at an early date. This was a laborious process that was not generally completed until 1927 because of the widespread economic dislocations that followed the war. In some cases the return to gold involved stabilisation of the currency at the pre-war parity, the most notable example being that of Great Britain in 1925. In other cases, such as that of France, Italy, and Belgium, currencies were repegged to gold at only a fraction of their pre-war parities. In those countries where hyperinflation had occurred in the early post-war years, notably in Germany, the stabilisation process necessitated the introduction of completely new currencies.

The international gold standard that was restored in the mid-1920s differed in several respects from that of the pre-1914 period. Apart from in the USA, the gold coin standard had virtually disappeared, and gold holdings remained predominantly in official hands. Several countries, including Great Britain, adopted a so-called gold bullion standard under which the currency was redeemable in gold but only in the form of bars of a minimum weight. This in effect made gold available only for purposes of settling international balances. The great majority of countries, partly in view of a prevailing belief in an actual or impending world shortage of gold, adopted varieties of the gold exchange standard.

International gold standard, which for the most part was a gold exchange standard, broke down in 1930 to 1932 under the impact of the world depression, the virtual cessation of international lending, the massive liquidation by central banks of their foreign exchange holdings, and the large-scale flights of capital from individual countries. Great Britain abandoned gold standard in September 1931 and USA suspended it in March 1933.

Gold Tranche **See International Monetary Fund**

Government Company

A Government company is a body corporate created under the general law as, for example, Indian Companies Act 1956. It embodies features of a private limited company with whole of the capital stock or 51 per cent or more owned by the Government. When the whole of the capital stock is not owned by the Government, the enterprise is sometimes described as joint company, provided the share of the Government is not less than 51 per cent of the stock capital. The directors are appointed by the Government and the employees of the company are not civil servants. It can sue and be sued. It is generally exempt from the personnel, budget, accounting and auditing laws and procedures applicable to Government departments.

Company form of organisation is considered advantageous because it allows flexibility and autonomy necessary for the successful operation of a commercial enterprise. However, in actual practice, most of the functions of a public sector company are vested in the Government and therefore the law regulating limited companies becomes a mere fiction.

Grants

Grants are unilateral transfers from one level of government to another (usually lower) level of government. They have the advantage of being targeted towards fiscally disadvantaged state/municipal governments to reduce horizontal fiscal imbalances. They can also be made conditional regarding their utilisation.

Keeping in mind the criteria of fiscal equity and efficiency, three types of grants may be given by a higher level government to a lower level government.

1. General purpose (or unconditional) grants are given to offset fiscal disadvantages arising from lower taxable capacity and/or higher unit cost of the services provided (due to bad terrain etc.). Such equalising grants have to be general and their basic purpose is to enable different municipalities to come up to a minimum standard of services provided.

2. Specific purpose (or conditional) grants are tied to the achievement of specific objectives. They may be with or without matching requirements. They are used to ensure minimum levels of specified public services to be provided by municipalities. Such grants are justified also where municipal services have spill over effects. Thus,

afforestation, slum improvement, and literacy drives create benefits not only for the local residents but also for the community as a whole. Such schemes should preferably be financed through grants from the state to municipalities.

3. Incentive grants are given for the purpose of encouraging municipalities to streamline their operations. These grants should depend on the measures taken by the municipalities to strengthen their financial position.

Great Chicken War

It refers to a trade war between the European Economic Community (EEC) and the USA during 1962-1965 over chicken imports from the latter. EEC imposed high tariffs on chicken imports from USA which, in retaliation, raised its tariff on imports of brandy, assembled trucks and few other items. Various efforts by GATT to diffuse this tariff war failed. As a result, poultry exports of USA to EEC contracted by about two-thirds. Accusations and threats were followed by counter accusations and threats.

Great Depression

In the early years of 1930s, USA and other capitalist countries of the world suffered a business depression of extraordinary severity. The demand for goods fell sharply and so also the prices. Many business firms failed and million of workers were rendered unemployed. These events revealed that something was seriously wrong with the working of a capitalist system. Out of the turmoil of depression came a book that had a profound effect on the thinking of economists. It was titled *The General Theory of Employment, Interest and Money* (1936) authored by British economist John Maynard Keynes (1883-1946). This work was immediately recognised as a revolutionary landmark in the history of economic ideas. See also Keynesian Economics.

Gresham's Law

Named after Sir Thomas Gresham (1519-1579), it states that bad money drives good money out of circulation. Bad money here means money whose intrinsic value is less than its face value while good money is that whose intrinsic value exceeds its face value.

Grey Market

It refers to a market in which commodities in short supply are sold for immediate delivery at exorbitant prices, taking unfair advantage of a crisis situation.

Gross Value Added at Market Prices See Value of Output

Group of Five (G-5)

It refers to five rich and powerful countries (USA, France, Japan, UK, and Germany) which meet periodically to co-ordinate their economic policies.

Group of Seven (G-7)

It refers to seven largest industrial countries of the world (USA, Canada, Japan, UK, Germany, France, and Italy) which meet from time to time to discuss contemporary economic policies and objectives.

Group of Ten (G-10)

It refers to a group of ten developed countries within the International Monetary Fund, viz. Belgium, Canada, France,

Germany, Italy, Japan, the Netherlands, Sweden, UK, and USA.

Growth Versus Equity

There is a school of thought which believes that highly unequal distribution of income is necessary for ensuring rapid economic growth. Take care of national output as this will take care of poverty, it is argued. However, this view has been challenged by American economist Michael Todaro and others. They believe that a development strategy focusing on reduction of income inequalities need not conflict with the objective of rapid growth.

Believers of conflict between growth and equity maintain that a highly skewed income distribution is a necessary condition for saving and investment. The assumption here is that the Marginal Propensity to Consume (q.v.) of the rich is low. Or, to put it differently, their Marginal Propensity to Save (q.v.) is high. Any addition to the already high personal and corporate incomes will be used mainly for saving/investment.

If income is taken away from the rich and distributed among the poor, the level of saving/investment in the economy would fall. Any additional income placed in the hands of the poor will be used for meeting consumption needs because the marginal propensity to consume of the poor classes is high, i.e. their marginal propensity to save is low. Thus, any income redistribution effort would lower growth rate.

According to Michael Todaro, the foregoing line of reasoning is an apology for the accumulation of wealth by powerful elite groups. There are several criticisms of the argument that skewed income distribution promotes saving/investment.

1. Unlike the historical experience of presently developed countries, the rich in less developed countries do not save and invest productivity. Instead they waste away much of their income on imported luxury goods, expensive houses, foreign travel, and gold and jewellery.

2. Low incomes of the poor lead to malnutrition, disease and lack of education and training. In other words, low standard of living reduces the productivity of workers and hence contributes to slower growth rate of the economy.

3. Reduction in mass poverty through more equitable distribution of income will provide material and psychological incentive to widespread public participation in the development process. It will stimulate local production, local employment and hence conditions for rapid economic growth.

In order to reduce inequalities and at the same time ensure accelerated growth, government intervention through a policy package is required. It may contain the following measures.

1. Producers should be encouraged to follow labour-intensive techniques of production. This can be done through public wage subsidies to private employers and/or tax concessions to labour-intensive units.

2. The principal reason for income inequalities in LDCs is the concentration of income-earning assets in few hands. As such, land reforms can act as a strong incentive to increase production and income for the vast majority of tenant cultivators converted into small holders of land.

3. Government can promote a wider access to educational opportunities for the poor. This, along with

employment opportunities, will help the poor to capitalise the benefits of modern knowledge.

4. Governments in LDCs can mobilise finance through income taxes, property taxes and inheritance taxes. These taxes have not proved effective in LDCs because there is widespread under-reporting/non-reporting of income and wealth by the rich. Conversely, taxes on commodities (excise duties, sales tax etc.) dominate governmental revenues. In many cases, necessities of life are also taxed and the burden of tax is borne by all sections of society, even by the poorest of the poor.

If revenue is raised from the rich and benefits of public expenditure are directed towards the poor, then fiscal policy can become a potent tool of redistributive objective. This can be done by initiating schemes which improve the productivity and earning capacity of the poor. Poor people must get priority in receiving benefits of subsidised/free educational, medical and housing facilities.

Many economists now believe that greater equality in LDCs may in fact be a condition for self-sustaining economic growth. However, there are serious political, institutional and power structure problems in following a development strategy favourable to the poor. There is also the practical question whether LDCs can switch over to such a strategy while remaining open to foreign aid, private foreign investment, imported technology and international demonstration effect.

H

Hard Currency See Currency

Hard-to-Tax Incomes

These are incomes which are not properly recorded and therefore are difficult to assess for the purpose of taxation. The three hard-to-tax classes of the non-corporate sector are: (a) unincorporated commercial and industrial units, (b) self-employed professionals and (c) rich peasantry. The problem of taxing the first two categories relates to accounting difficulties while in the case of third category, it is essentially the lack of political will. Non-reporting and under-reporting of income is quite sizeable in these sectors. The small business sector is a tax haven because it is very difficult to enforce a reliable system of book-keeping to assess earnings of this sector. Pragmatically, a system of presumptive taxation may be tried in place of regular assessment of income. See also Soft-to-Tax Incomes.

Heads of Income

Income tax is generally a composite tax on the aggregate of incomes from various sources. However, income is first computed under different heads of income and then aggregated. From the aggregated amount certain deductions are made to arrive at taxable income.

For example, Section 14 of the Indian Income Tax Act, 1961, prescribes five broad heads under which income of an assessee is classified for the purpose of computation of total income and the charge of income tax. These are: 1. Salaries,

2. Income from house property, 3. Profits and gains of business or profession, 4. Capital gains, and 5. Income from other sources. These five heads of income are mutually exclusive. If any income falls under one head, it cannot be considered under any other head.

Heckscher-Ohlin Theory of Trade

The Ricardian theory of comparative advantage in trade assumes one factor of production i.e. labour. Differences in the productivity of labour are considered the cause for international trade.

According to Heckscher-Ohlin theory of trade, the reason for international trade lies in differences in factor endowments of different countries. The theory assumes two factors of production viz., labour and capital. Some countries are endowed with abundance of labour while some countries have abundance of capital. Heckscher-Ohlin theory states that countries which are capital-abundant (or labour scarce) will export capital-intensive goods while labour-abundant (or capital-scarce) countries will export labour-intensive goods.

Heckscher-Ohlin theory is based on the following assumptions:

1. There are no transport costs or other barriers to trade.

2. There is perfect competition in commodity as well as in factor market.

3. All production functions are homogenous of the first degree.

4. The production functions are such that the two commodities show different factor intensities. It means that different techniques of production are used in the two industries.

5. The production functions differ between commodities, but are the same in both countries. It means the best technique of production is known to all participating countries.

The assumption of Heckscher-Ohlin theory are very restrictive. They are rarely fulfilled in the real world. This makes the theory less relevant to the practical problems of international trade.

Hedging

It is a method to guard against fluctuations in the prices of commodities (particularly raw materials) scheduled for future delivery by dealing in futures market. *Buying hedge* and *selling hedge* are the two basic types of hedge operations.

High-powered Money

It is composed of cash in the hands of the public, bank reserves and clearing balances held by the commercial banks with the central bank.

Highway-user Tax

It is a tax levied on the users of highways. The revenue is generally reserved for the construction and maintenance of highways. In USA, highway-user taxes are imposed by both the Federal and the State Governments. They are in the form of a fixed amount per gallon of gasoline sold, and licence fee for motor vehicles.

Hoarding

It refers to an act of accumulation. Dishoarding is the reverse of it, signifying spending.

Holding Company

It is a public authority entrusted with the task of general development and running of undertakings in a particular sector of industry. For example, Steel Authority of India Limited (SAIL) is a holding company.

Horizontal Compensation **See Loss Set Off**

Horizontal Equity

It is a tax equity criterion advocating similar tax treatment of persons in similar economic circumstances. See also Ability-to-Pay Principle of Taxation.

Horizontal Foreign Investment

Investment by a parent company (MNC) in the production of a similar or identical commodity in another country is known as a horizontal investment.

Hot Money

The term refers to money which can be transferred rapidly from one financial centre to another to take advantage of differences in short-term interest rates.

Hyperinflation

It is a situation when prices are rising extraordinarily fast, say doubling every week. Hyperinflation results in the disruption of normal economic activities, depreciation of currency and eventual breakdown of the entire monetary system.

Hypothesis

It is a statement about how two or more variables are related to each other. For example, it is a basic hypothesis in economics that demand for a commodity is inversely related to its price. Thus, as the price of sugar increases, its demand falls and vice versa. Empirical observations can either prove or refute hypotheses.

I

Impact of Tax

It refers to the point at which the burden of a tax falls initially. See also Incidence of Taxation.

Imperfect Competition See Monopolistic Competition

Implicit Cost See Cost of Production

Import Coefficient See Average Propensity to Import

Import Duty See Customs Duty

Imports

Imports are defined as goods taken into one country from another country in the conduct of foreign trade, with the first country being the importer and the second the exporter.

Import Substitution Effect

When tariff is imposed on import of a commodity, its price rises in the importing country enabling domestic producers to compete with it. Increase in domestic production of import substitutes or replacement of foreign production with domestic production in the post-tariff period is called import substitution effect of tariff.

Imputed Income

Imputed income arises when a taxpayer is himself the producer and the consumer of a given commodity or service.

Although no market transaction is involved yet the taxpayer enjoys a certain amount of consumption. There are two difficulties with imputed incomes: (a) they accrue in kind and (b) they are not the result of a market transaction.

Self-consumption enjoyed by the people allows them to economise on consumption expenditure in the market. A major item of imputed income which tax laws generally take into account relates to imputed income of owner-occupied houses. The owner could have rented his house to a tenant and earned taxable income. The rental income foregone represents consumption on the part of the owner occupying his house. Exemption of the services of a house in which owner lives rent-free will be discrimination in favour of occupying owners and against tenants. Imputed income from owner-occupied houses is computed on notional basis taking into account the actual rent of houses of similar size, location and quality.

Minor items of imputed income are generally ignored by tax laws, e.g. home-grown agricultural products (fruit and vegetables) which are not marketed but self-consumed. It is difficult for tax authorities to obtain their cash worth and include them in the taxable base. Self-consumption of agricultural produce is widespread in poor countries. It is neither desirable (on equity considerations) nor practicable (on administrative grounds) to tax such imputed incomes.

If one is to stretch the argument, many more items will have to be included in the tax net including the self-use of household durables. Further still, imputed income from the wife's services to the family should also be included in the taxable base. As William Vickrey has remarked, "If two housewives were to do each other's work for pay, the income under present laws would be greater than if they each do their own work." The domain of imputed incomes is ambiguous and stretchable to ridiculous limits. Tax administrators are the better judges to draw the dividing line taking into account ground realities of the situation. The sheer inability to measure most types of non-market sources of income leads to their exclusion from the taxable base. It can cause distortions by encouraging taxpayers to substitute non-market for market activities.

Incidence of Taxation

It refers to the final resting place of tax burden as against the impact which means the first place where a tax is imposed. The incidence of a tax is on the person who ultimately pays it, i.e. who cannot shift it any further.

Due to economic transactions, a tax percolates through many parts of the economy and the burden of it can be shifted, forward or backward, by the original taxpayer to other entities.

When taxes are imposed, disposable real incomes of the people get reduced. Real incomes may be reduced either because there is reduction in disposable money income (direct taxes) or because the prices of products purchased are enhanced (indirect taxes). The disposable real income of a household is subject to both direct and indirect tax effects. The total incidence of a tax system on an individual is equal to the sum of tax burden borne by him as a producer and as a consumer.

For every rupee raised as tax, there is a corresponding reduction in the disposable real income of someone or another. Reduction in one's disposable real income is taken to be equivalent to the tax realisation by the government. Incidence analysis pertains to tracking down individuals or households whose real incomes are truncated when taxes are imposed. Incidence analysis deals with the diffusion of tax burden among different economic classes in a country.

Statutory Versus Economic Incidence: Persons who have legal responsibility of paying taxes to the government suffer statutory incidence (or impact) of a tax. In other words, statutory incidence refers to the legal placing of the tax liability, i.e. who bears the tax burden in the first instance. For example, the statutory incidence of excise duty on sugar is on the producer of sugar.

Those who suffer statutory incidence of a tax are not necessarily the ultimate bearers of the tax burden. Very often, persons who have the legal obligation of paying taxes to government shift, in part or in full, the tax burden to consumers or other entities. This shifting becomes possible through economic transactions in an economy. Hence, those who bear the tax burden ultimately suffer the economic incidence of a tax. It refers to the final resting place of a tax. If excise duty on sugar is shifted by the producers on to the consumers, the latter suffer the economic incidence of the duty.

Absolute Versus Relative Incidence: The extent to which persons in different economic groups are hurt as a result of the imposition of taxes is generally measured in terms of money burden of taxes as a percentage of money income/expenditure of various groups. Thus, the amount of income surrendered as taxes by the income receivers is the absolute measure of tax burden while the proportion of income paid as taxes is a relative measure of this burden. Obviously, it is the relative burden which is relevant for comparing money burden of taxes on households in different income/expenditure groups.

Formal Versus Effective Incidence: Formal incidence means the money burden of taxes as resting with subject on whom the burden is intended by the tax authority to fall. In other words, it refers to the statistical estimate of tax payments by income groups.

In addition to imposing direct money burden (formal incidence), taxes generate certain effects which may affect the relative economic positions of individuals and households. Effective incidence refers to the economic effects of taxation.

Differential Tax Incidence: It relates to the study of the effects of a tax that has been substituted for another tax yielding equal revenue. See also Shifting of Tax.

Income

It is indeed very difficult to reduce the concept of income to a precise and unambiguous definition. Various forms of imputed and accrued incomes pose serious practical difficulties of measurement. Guidance is often sought from judicial pronouncements on the subject.

In the income tax laws of most countries, income is exemplified rather than defined. For example, Section 2 (24) of the Indian Income Tax Act, 1961, describes various receipts as income which include, *inter alia*, the following: profits and gains, dividends, voluntary contributions received by a charitable trust, value of any perquisite or profit in lieu of salary, any capital gains, winnings from lotteries, crossword puzzles etc.

Apart from the aforesaid receipts, any other receipt is taxable under the Act if it comes within the general and natural connotation of the term *income*. Thus, the law brings under charge various types of income which may be classified as follows: (a) income received, (b) income deemed to be received, e.g. annual accretion to the account of an employee participating in a recognised provident fund, dividend declared by a company but not yet received by individual shareholder (c) income accrued, and (d) income deemed to have accrued. Income is said to be received when it reaches the assessee. It is said to accrue or arise when the right to receive the income becomes vested in the assessee. In short, the description of the term *income* in Section 2 (24) is inclusive and not exclusive. See also Net Accretion Theory of Income.

Income Averaging

Income may arise either as a regular flow, e.g. salary of a college teacher or as an irregular flow like earnings of a theatre artist, gambling or lottery gains. All such accretions represent taxpaying capacity of the recipient and therefore should form part of the tax base. However, fluctuating incomes are discriminated against under a progressive rate schedule because high marginal rates apply in years of high income. Contrarily, stable income is free from fluctuating marginal rates and hence favourably treated.

Tax systems generally make direct or indirect (proxy) provisions of averaging of incomes over several years. These provisions may take the form of higher rebates, and higher deductions from income for those whose incomes are subject to fluctuations. See also Loss Set Off; Loss Carry Back; and Loss Carry Forward.

Income Elasticity of Demand

Income elasticity of demand is the ratio of percentage change in demand to percentage change in income.

$$Ey = \frac{\text{Percentage change in demand}}{\text{Percentage change in income}}$$

If there is a decrease in the demand for a commodity when income increases, the income elasticity of that commodity will be negative. This type of commodity will be called an inferior good. If income elasticity is positive, the commodity in question is a normal one. Generally speaking, if Ey > 1, the normal commodity is a luxury, otherwise it is a necessity.

Income Tax

It is a tax levied on the annual income of various taxable entities, mainly individuals and companies. The taxable income is determined after taking into account certain exemptions and deductions. No tax at all is paid on a basic income that is exempt.

Rate schedule of the tax is generally progressive. The larger the taxable income, the higher the tax rate. Higher rates apply not to the total income but to increments of income. The progressive nature of income tax is based on the Ability-to-Pay Principle of Taxation (q.v.).

Income Tax and Inflation: Income tax law in most countries is defined in terms of monetary units with progressive rates. Combined with progressive rate schedule, inflation has a tendency to increase real tax burden and change its incidence across taxpaying classes. This, in the ultimate analysis, impairs the equity attribute of a tax system.

Inflation-Induced Distortions: If the money income of an individual grows at the same rate as inflation, he might be pushed into the tax orbit although his real income remains constant. How inflation distorts the tax code approved by legislators may be understood by an example. Suppose an individual with a total income of Rs. 40,000 per annum has no tax liability and the income in excess of Rs. 40,000 is subject to tax at the rate of 20 per cent. Allowing for a price rise of 10 per cent in period II over period I, the money income of the individual would be Rs. 44,000 in period II if his income increases proportionately with the price rise. As a result, he will become liable to pay tax of 20 per cent on the excess of total income above Rs. 40,000. With tax liability amounting to Rs. 800 his post-tax income falls to Rs. 43,200 whose real value in terms of period I is only Rs. 39,273. Although no change takes place in the tax structure and the real income, the individual is made to part with Rs. 800 in money terms or Rs. 727 in real terms. All this happens quietly through fiscal illusion.

By the same token, inflation may push an assessee from a lower to a higher income and tax bracket. In the case of a proportional tax, the marginal rates of tax remain the same for all income brackets and therefore real tax burden remains constant in the event of a rise in money income. In practice, however, the rates are not proportional but progressive. Since the marginal tax rates increase with rising money income, individuals, when forced into higher income slab with higher rate, are obliged to make higher tax payments reducing their net of tax income in real terms.

Real burden of taxes increases not merely because of the progressive rate schedule but also because of the changing real values of exemptions and deductions designed in nominal fixed amounts. Assuming a proportional tax for all income brackets, the taxpayers will be worse off in real terms if the amount of exemptions and deductions does not increase or increases less than proportionately to the rate of inflation.

Another important effect of inflation on the tax rate schedule is to shrink the real width of tax brackets. The width of the tax brackets generally increases with increasing incomes and becomes an open-end class ultimately. As against this, rate differentials become narrower at higher tax brackets. Thus, individuals with higher incomes are insulated against the effects of inflation because either they remain in the same tax bracket or if at all they move to a higher tax bracket, the rate differential is not significant. Taxpayers whose incomes are already subject to maximum rate of tax are fully protected against the effects of inflation.

Inflation and progression in tax rates affect each level of income to an extent that depends on the rate of progression at that income. This means inflation-induced tax increases are highest not at incomes where the marginal tax rates are highest, but at incomes where marginal tax rates increase most sharply. Thus, it is clear that inflationary tax increases fall most heavily on low-income taxpayers with incomes just below or above the exemption level where width of income brackets is small but marginal tax rates increase rapidly. It is this class of taxpayers which needs protection against the onslaughts of inflation.

It should particularly be noted that by increasing the money incomes of the low-income groups, inflation pushes these groups into the tax net. When an individual is pushed into the taxpaying category, he finds his marginal rate of tax suddenly jumping from zero to say 20 per cent. The hike is generally larger than that experienced by individuals moving from a lower to a higher slab in the wake of inflation.

In brief, inflation, by upsetting the initial tax code given by the legislators, impairs the progressivity of tax structure. It changes the decisions of the law makers effectively and irresponsibly without public debate. Real income tax rates increase during inflation although the formal tax structure remains the same. Moreover, changes in the real tax rates, induced by inflation, are of a permanent nature. After a while, further price rise may stop but the shift introduced by inflation in real income tax rates will stay on for subsequent period.

Corrective Measures: To mitigate (or offset) the unintended tax burden induced by inflation and the resultant anomalies in the distribution of tax burden, the following measures may be adopted. The purpose of these adjustments is to ensure that each level of income is taxed in real terms at approximately the same rate as originally intended, i.e. in the base year. In other words, the objective is to preserve the tax structure in real terms rather than in monetary terms. The original tax code may be taken to reflect a socially desired distribution of tax burden and if it is to be maintained through time, the need for an adjustment mechanism appears to be justified in equity terms. If, however, the initial situation becomes unsatisfactory, it would be preferable to make any desired changes explicitly rather than to rely on the ambiguous influence of inflation.

Periodic Adjustments: To deal with the distortionary effects of inflation, governments usually make adjustments to exemptions and tax brackets at the beginning of a current year on the basis of inflation experienced in a previous period. The difficulty with this procedure is that frequent periodic changes in income tax laws are likely to cause legal complications and procedural problems. Efficiency of tax administration is reduced as the officers have to spend considerable time keeping themselves up-to-date with changes in law. Moreover, such adjustments are irregular and may not eliminate the effects of inflation to ensure continuance of the given real tax burden and its distribution.

Automatic Adjustment Schemes: Alternatively, automatic adjustment schemes may be adopted to protect incomes against the problems created by the combination of inflation and progressivity in income tax rates. Such schemes, in one form or the other, have been adopted in many countries to combat distortionary effects of inflation on tax structure.

Under one type of scheme, known as the real income adjustment scheme, tax structure is left untouched but taxpayers are allowed to adjust their income by some inflationary factor. For this method, the procedure could be as follows. Tax structure is defined in terms of constant rupees (say 1990-91 = 100). Current income of the taxpayer is expressed in terms of the base year prices. Tax liability is computed in terms of base year income. By multiplying base year tax liability by the ratio of the price index of the taxable year to the price index of the base year, tax liability in terms of current prices is obtained. In other words, this scheme involves calculation of tax on real income in some base year and the determination of the current liability by converting this amount to current prices.

Schemes have also been devised under which tax rates are altered through indexation while keeping income brackets unchanged. Rates and brackets are defined by law, and each year the government has to declare the proportions to which these basic rates apply. In other words, having defined the basic rates in law, the effective rates are fixed annually when the government establishes a coefficient of adjustment.

Under yet another scheme, adjustments are made in the tax structure only for inflation above a certain level. For example, the income tax indexation law of California in the United States, which incidentally was the first state to enact such a law in 1978, allows adjustments in the tax rates only for inflation above the first 3 per cent level. Such a scheme, called partial indexation, may mitigate effects of inflation but it does not eliminate them. Partial indexation of this type fails to deal with slow inflation. After several years of moderate inflation, the tax structure could seriously get distorted. Also, the more even the inflation over the years, the less will be the benefit to taxpayers. For example, if the rate of inflation is 3 per cent per annum for two consecutive years, no adjustment will be made. However, if it is zero in one year and 6 per cent in the other year, the adjustment will be of the order of 3 per cent.

Corrective measures to offset the adverse inflationary effects are required particularly when inflation persists for longer periods. Introduction of some form of inflation adjustment scheme will require legislative approval only once and will be more equitable and in conformity with the basic philosophy underlying progressive taxation. This kind of adjustment will not only stabilise incomes of individuals in real terms but also government revenues.

There are few relatively weak arguments against indexation. For example, it is argued that indexation neutralises the built-in-flexibility which is a desirable characteristic of a progressive tax system. Rising tax revenues automatically moderate growth in aggregate demand and thus ensure stabilisation. This argument may hold good in the initial stages of inflation but loses significance when high rates of inflation persist for longer periods. A stage may come when taxpayers start demanding increase in money wages not only to offset the decrease in the value of money but also to nullify the effects of inflation on tax burden. Inflation adjustments, by preventing tax-push inflation, may promote rather than impair the stabilisation function of a tax system.

Inflation indexing schemes, though technically sound, may appear to be radical measures in developing countries. The acceptability of such schemes will depend upon proper understanding of the relationship between inflation and taxes.

Income Tax and Labour Supply: How does an increase in income tax affect the incentive and efficiency to work of a taxpayer? Reduced income due to increased taxation may decrease his efficiency but this must be set against the increase in efficiency due to benefits of public expenditure.

Whether less or more work will be done by a taxpayer after enhanced taxation will depend upon his elasticity of demand for money. If to earn a particular level of income is compulsory for him (i.e. demand for money is inelastic), an increase in tax will force him to work for longer hours. Under normal circumstances, he may slacken his efforts to enjoy greater leisure (substitution effect) or he may intensify his efforts to recoup the erosion of purchasing power on account of higher tax (income effect). The net result will depend on the relative strength of these two opposite forces. It is indeed difficult to evaluate the two effects and their net result.

Generally, the supply of labour as regards married women is more responsive to the level of net earnings, than is the case for men. According to J.A. Kay, "A current consensus, however, suggests that substitution effects are generally large for secondary earners (particularly married women) but that the earnings/leisure substitution elasticity is generally small for male principal earners.... Just as the effect of income tax on labour supply is ambiguous, so is the influence of a tax on capital income on savings." See also Corporate Income Tax; and Basic Exemption.

Increasing Returns to Scale See Returns to Scale

Incremental Capital-Output Ratio

It signifies relationship between investment and additional output during a particular period. In other words, it is a summary expression for the existing technical conditions which determine the relationship between investment and additional output in an economy. See also Capital-Output Ratio.

Indemnity Payments

These refer to transfer of funds from one government to another as compensation for losses due to any reason, but primarily due to war. There is no subsequent counter flow of capital for indemnity payments.

Indifference Curve

The theory of consumption explains how a consumer gets maximum satisfaction from out of his limited income. British economist Alfred Marshall (1842-1924) explained it with the help of his law of equi-marginal utility. As an alternative to Marshallian explanation, another British economist J. R. Hicks suggested indifference curve technique to determine consumer's equilibrium. An indifference curve shows various combinations of commodities X and Y which give an individual the same level of satisfaction. See also Diminishing Marginal Rate of Substitution.

Indirect Tax

It is a tax which can be shifted from the original payer to the ultimate consumer of the commodity or service taxed. Import duties, excise levies, and sales taxes are generally regarded as indirect taxes. Thus, an excise duty on cigarettes levied on producers is usually passed on to the consumers in the form of higher prices.

Indirect taxes (also called hidden taxes) are convenient to collect but lack equity attribute. They do not allow considerations for the personal circumstances of taxpayers as do direct taxes. It is not possible to grant exemptions or allow deductions or to have a progressive rate schedule. Indirect taxes are borne in relation to the consumption expenditure which constitutes a higher percentage of income for lower income groups than for persons in higher income brackets. It is true that incidence of indirect taxes depends on (a) the selection of commodities for taxation and (b) the rate of tax on them. It is desirable that luxuries and comforts are chosen for heavy taxation with necessities of life either exempted or moderately taxed. However, in poor countries the demand for luxury items is limited apart from being price elastic. Conversely, the demand for necessities is vast and price inelastic, obliging tax authorities to extend the tax net to daily needs. This has a tendency to fuel inflation.

In short, it is almost universally accepted that indirect taxes are inferior to direct taxes in terms of equity attribute.

The distribution of indirect tax burden is often, though not always, regressive and even the poorest of the poor are made to contribute to public exchequer. See also Direct Tax; Incidence of Taxation; and Tax Shifting.

Inductive Reasoning **See Deductive and Inductive Reasoning**

Industrial Finance

Modern system of industrial production is very complex requiring huge investments both in terms of material and human resources. It may be beyond the capacity of an individual to arrange on his own all the resources required to undertake production. Modern corporations or joint stock companies are the answer to these requirements.

Financial needs of a modern industry may be classified into two categories: (a) fixed capital and (b) working capital. Modern industry is capital-intensive by nature and its fixed capital includes lands and buildings, plant and machinery, and tools and implements. The requirement of finance to purchase fixed capital is essentially long-term in nature. The working capital, short-term in nature, is required to purchase raw materials and meet day-to-day administrative and other such expenses.

There are various sources of finance for a modern industrial unit. These sources are of two types: (a) internal sources and (b) external sources. Internal sources include paid-up capital in the form of share subscriptions, ploughing back of profits, and reserves. The external sources include debenture issue, public deposits, loans from commercial banks and other specialised institutions.

Industrial Revolution

It started in the middle of the 18th century in Britain and gradually spread to other European countries. Industrial revolution implies the onset of fundamental changes in the structure of an economy, particularly redeployment of resources away from agriculture. Each industrial revolution contains the following essential ingredients: (a) shift from family-based subsistence units of production to the impersonal capitalistic form of enterprise, (b) opening up of national and international markets for goods and factors of production, (c) use of machines, (d) use of new raw materials which are either more efficient or less scarce and (e) shift from primary production to secondary and tertiary production.

Infant Industry Argument

According to this argument for tariff protection, some industries have the potentiality to grow and earn comparative advantage only if they are protected from foreign competition in their infancy. Therefore, competitive imports should be taxed or curbed. Once these industries grow and mature, they can face competition and then the protection can be withdrawn. See also Bastable Test.

Inflation

Inflation means a significant rise in the general price level in a country over a long period of time. Inflation is the opposite of price stability. In economics, price stability is not used in a rigid sense to mean price fixity. A modest increase of 2 to 3 per cent in the price level per annum is compatible, sometimes even desirable, with the general connotation of price stability. However, when the general price rise is appreciable, say in double-digit figure, and experienced over a long period of time, it gets the dreaded name inflation.

Changes in the level of prices are measured by means of index numbers. The index of prices includes a wide variety of goods and services which are essential for life. Since the relative importance of different goods in the family budget is not the same therefore each commodity included in the index is assigned a weight in accordance with the proportion of family expenditure on that commodity. The prices of different commodities multiplied by their respective weights give the aggregate for the year chosen as the base. This is then compared with the similar aggregate of prices in some subsequent year for the purpose of comparison. The base year is changed from time to time to accommodate new products and reflect current economic conditions.

Analysis of price variations is essential to understand the general economic conditions and the value of money in the economy. Price fluctuations influence (a) the distribution of income among various economic classes and (b) the allocation of resources among competing sectors. Hence, their analysis indicates as to what regulatory policies by the government are needed as corrective measures. Price stability is a pre-requisite for a successful development strategy.

Pressure on prices is a manifestation of macro-imbalance between demand for and supply of commodities and services. Inflation signifies excess of demand for goods and services over their available supply. It is a case of too much money chasing too few goods.

The reasons for excess of demand over supply are many. Demand may expand due to any combination of the following factors: (a) increase in population leading to increased demand for essential items, (b) increase in government expenditure, particularly when it is met by deficit financing and the consequent monetary expansion, (c) increase in private conspicuous consumption due to tax evasion and violation of economic regulations.

Supply may lag behind demand due to (a) unfavourable and uncertain weather conditions, (b) outmoded technology and (c) lack of infrastructural facilities.

The distortionary effects of inflation are injurious to the smooth functioning of an economy. Therefore, price stability is a prime concern of the governments the world over. Excessive price rise causes economic distortions and social unrest, threatening political stability. Price stability is, therefore, at the root of socio-politico orderliness.

Fluctuations in the general level of prices cause corresponding changes in the value or purchasing power of money. When prices are high, the value of money is low and vice versa. Fluctuating price level causes major disturbances in the economy. Rising prices adversely affect the economic conditions of fixed income groups, particularly wage-earners. There is always a lag between price rise and money wage adjustment. Poor people in the unorganised sector are hit the worst because their incomes are not linked with price index. However, the business firms gain during price rise because the money value of goods in their stock rises continually.

Fluctuating prices generate opposite effects on debtors and creditors. Rising prices prove beneficial for debtors at the expense of creditors. Thus, inflation discourages people to invest in financial assets. Conversely, falling prices make it difficult for debtors to meet their obligations.

Judicious demand and supply management policies are required to counteract inflationary tendencies. The main elements of strategy on the demand side include restrictive monetary policy and control of public and private expenditure.

Supply management includes fuller utilisation of and addition to existing capacities. This would require adequate and timely availability of power, raw materials and transport facilities.

Inflationary Gap

It is a situation in which the actual national income of a country exceeds its potential income.

Inflation Tax

There are several ways through which resources can be acquired by the government for public use. One such method is deficit financing, i.e. printing more currency. Through deficit financing, it can purchase a part of goods and services available in the economy. Since such a policy usually leads to price rise, it is called *inflation tax*. The effects of such a policy are very disorderly in the sense that the burden of inflation falls inequitably on different classes.

Inheritance Tax

It is a levy on persons who receive property upon the death of a benefactor. It is different from Estate Duty (q.v.) which is based on the value of the entire estate left behind by a decedent and before it is divided among the heirs. A tax on each inheritance to which the estate gives rise is known as inheritance tax or succession duty.

Ability-to-pay principle provides theoretical justification for the imposition of inheritance tax because a bequest of property creates an ability on the part of the inheritor to contribute to public exchequer. The tax is justified because it prevents the formation of a permanent moneyed group which can live on property handed down from generation to generation.

Inheritance taxes are generally progressive. The rate of tax increases as the relationship of the heir to the deceased grows more remote. There are usually fairly high exemptions from the tax.

Innovations Theory of Profit **See Profit**

Input-Output Analysis

Input-output analysis, attributed to American economist Wassily Loentief deals with general equilibrium situation in the empirical study of production. It has three distinctive features: (a) it deals almost exclusively with production, (b) it is concerned with empirical investigations, (c) it is related to general equilibrium phenomenon.

Input-output analysis examines the interdependence of the production plans and activities of the various industries which constitute an economy. This interdependence arises because each industry employs the outputs of other industries, and its own output in turn is used by other industries. For example, steel is used to make railway wagons and railway wagons are in turn used to transport steel.

An input-output transaction matrix is a framework of data which provides a detailed information on how the final demand for output is related to the requirements placed on individual industries. It thus, highlights the interdependence of various economic sectors (industries) in the production of final output for the economy as a whole.

It is an array of rows and columns forming a square matrix. For each industry, the row displays the credit side of the production account, i.e. sales to other industries plus sales to final users. The column for the industry displays the debit side, i.e. purchase of materials and services from other industries plus purchases of factor services and non-factor charges. For each industry, the sum of row items equals the sum of the column items. Thus, for each industry total output produced equals the total inputs (including the non-factor charges). It should be noted that in the input-output transaction matrix the productive units of an economy are grouped into separate clusters to form a certain number of industries. Since in these groups all the productive units are covered, input-output transaction matrix encompasses all the productive activity within an economy.

There are various uses of input-output analysis to solve real world problems. It can be used in predicting future production requirements if demand estimates are available. It can be used for economic planning, including problems of backward areas of a country. Moreover, it provides useful information for national income accounting.

There are two important assumptions of input-output analysis. Firstly, no two commodities are produced jointly. In other words, each industry produces only one homogeneous output. Secondly, in any productive process all inputs are employed in rigidly fixed proportions and the use of these inputs expands in proportion with the level of output. This is a special case of an assumption of constant returns to scale. Input-output analysis requires the solution of a set of N simultaneous linear equations in N variables.

Intangible Asset **See Asset**

Intellectual Property Rights (IPR)

Any innovation, invention or improvement is the intellectual property of the person who undertakes it. He can get his property legally registered through patent, trade mark or copyright. This gives him a sole right to use his idea in whatever way he deems fit or sell it at the price/royalty he thinks suitable.

In recent years, the area of IPR has seen lot of interest emerging around it. Attempts are being made by various administrative bodies to strengthen these rights and minimise their theft, leakage or unauthorised usage.

Inter-corporate Dividends

These are dividends received by a company from another company. Income tax laws generally treat a parent (or a holding) company and its subsidiary company as separate legal entities and therefore tax them separately. Thus, if a holding company receives dividends from its subsidiary, the former has to pay tax on such dividends. Taxation of inter-corporate earnings is designed to prevent concentration of economic power in the hands of corporate giants. However, this provision is said to give rise to treble taxation of such dividends, first in the hands of the earning company, then in the hands of the receiving company, and finally in the hands of individual shareholders. Tax laws often provide certain concessions to facilitate inter-corporate investment.

In India, prior to the assessment year 1991-92, the adverse situation was partially remedied by Section 80M of the Income Tax Act, 1961, under which a company was entitled to a deduction of 60 per cent of dividend received by it from another domestic company. An important change was introduced from the assessment year 1991-92 under which dividends received by a domestic company from another domestic company are now exempt to the full extent to which the assessee company itself distributes dividends during the relevant period. Business community has complained that this arrangement has forced companies to declare dividends. It favours complete exemption of inter-corporate dividends from tax.

Interest

Interest is defined as a payment made or received for the use of money. It is calculated as a percentage of the principal amount, payable annually. Rate of interest is important because it affects saving and investment decisions of the people in an economy.

Gross and Net Interest: Gross interest means the rate of interest actually charged in the loan market. However, the lender has to spend some money to maintain accounts and collect payment of interest. If the lender is to be compensated for all these administrative expenses, the gross rate will be somewhat above the net rate which is actually available to him. Thus,

Net interest = Gross interest - Administrative costs.

Real and Money Rate of Interest: Money rate of interest is calculated simply in terms of money paid. Real rate of interest pertains to the ratio of the purchasing power of money returned to the purchasing power of money borrowed. This distinction is important in the context of inflationary pressures in the economy. Real rate of interest is the difference between the money rate of interest and the rate of inflation. For example, if the money rate of interest is 15 per cent and the inflation rate is 10 per cent, the real rate of interest is 5 per cent. If inflation rate is 18 per cent, the real rate is -3 per cent.

How is Interest Rate Determined? Among the various explanations provided by economists for the determination of the rate of interest, the following two are important: (a) loanable fund theory and (b) liquidity preference theory. They are explained below.

Loanable Fund Theory of the Rate of Interest: Loanable fund theory is attributed to Swedish economist Knut Wicksell (1851-1926) and the British economist Dennis Robertson (1890-1963). According to this theory, the rate of interest is determined by the demand for and the supply of loanable funds in an economy. It is based on the assumption of perfect competition. The demand for loans originates from three types of borrowers, viz. producers, consumers and government. Producers borrow in order to make investment in industrial and commercial activities. Consumers borrow primarily for financing the purchase of durable consumer goods. Government borrows to finance public works (roads, bridges etc.) in peace-time and to meet emergencies like a war.

Adding up the demand for loans by producers, consumers and the government, a combined demand curve for loans is obtained. Like any other demand curve, it slopes downward, signifying that lower the rate of interest, greater the demand for loans and vice versa.

Supply of loans comes from the current savings of households as well as business firms. These savings are channelled through commercial banks, insurance companies and other financial institutions. They are made available to various types of borrowers. Adding up the personal and business savings, a combined supply curve is obtained which, like any other supply curve, slopes upwards, denoting that lower the rate of interest, the lower the supply of loans and vice versa. By bringing together the demand and supply curves of loanable funds, one can see the determination of the rate of interest at the point where the two curves intersect.

Loanable fund theory is a very simplistic explanation of an otherwise complex phenomenon. In real world, rate of interest is influenced by a host of subjective and objective factors.

Liquidity Preference Theory of the Rate of Interest: According to British economist John Maynard Keynes (1883-1946) rate of interest is a reward for parting with liquidity for a specified period of time. Rate of interest, he believed, is a purely monetary phenomenon determined by the demand for and supply of money (liquidity).

The supply of money is given by the government, i.e. it is an exogenous (or autonomous) factor and accepted as it is. However, the demand for money (or preference for liquidity) varies and hence plays active role in the determination of the rate of interest.

Why do people demand money (i.e. liquidity) when they know that holding of cash does not earn them any interest income? If wealth can be held in the form of interest-earning bonds why hold it in the form of cash? Keynes explained public preference for liquidity in terms of the following three motives.

Transactions Motive: People prefer to hold some money for meeting current transactions of daily life.

Precautionary Motive: People hold liquidity to provide for contingencies requiring sudden expenditure, e.g. accident, illness etc.

According to Keynes, the demand for liquidity for transaction and precautionary motives (labelled L_1) is positively related to the level of income. It is generally a fixed proportion of an individual's income. Thus, $L_1 = kY$.

Speculative Motive: People may hold surplus cash over and above what is required to satisfy transaction and precautionary motives. Keynes called this extra demand for liquidity (labelled L_2) as speculative demand for money for speculative motive. It arises due to fluctuations of interest rates and uncertainty about them. Thus, it is a function of the rate of interest, $L_2 = f(r)$. We assume that the normal expected rate of interest is 10 per cent and the bonds also carry 10 per cent rate of interest. If the actual market rate of interest falls below the normal rate, the bond prices will lie above their normal price because there is inverse relationship between bond prices and interest rates. In such a situation people in general will expect rate of interest to rise (i.e. bond prices to fall) in the near future. Bond holders would like to sell their bonds now at their high price and hold cash with a view to repurchase bonds when their prices fall to normal (i.e. rate of interest rises to normal). In this process they expect to make capital gains. Thus, individuals prefer to hold cash rather than bonds when the rate of interest is low relative to their expectations. The reverse holds when actual rate of interest lies above the normal rate (i.e. bond prices are below their normal price). Thus, Keynesian theory postulates a negative relationship between interest rate and the speculative demand for cash.

Keynsian theory assumes that different people have different expectations about future interest rates (or bond prices). There are two types of speculators in the market, the bulls and the bears. Bulls are those who expect the bond prices to rise in the future while bears are those who anticipate fall in bond prices. Thus, bulls invest all their surplus cash in bonds whereas bears move out of bonds into cash. Therefore, the speculative demand for liquidity arises from bears. These bears accumulate their cash reserves to purchase bonds when either bond prices have fallen as expected or when they start anticipating that bond prices will rise in future.

Determination of Rate of Interest

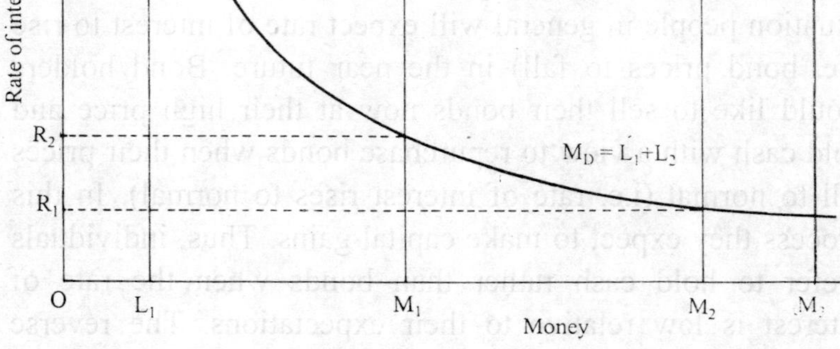

In the above diagram, the demand for money (liquidity) is represented by the downward-sloping curve labelled MD = $L_1 + L_2$. L_1 component of the total demand represents the demand for money for transaction and precautionary motives. It is assumed to be independent of the rate of interest and instead may be considered a fixed proportion of the income level. It is shown by the vertical line L_1 in the Figure below.

L_2 represents demand for liquidity for speculative motive which depends on the rate of interest. If we subtract L_1 from the M_D curve horizontally, the M_D curve becomes L_2 curve when read with L_1 as the origin instead of O.

Since money supply is determined by monetary authorities, it can be considered as fixed at a particular time. The supply curve of money is parallel to the vertical axis. In the Figure below, three alternative supplies of money have been shown at M_1 M_2 and M_3 .

The demand curve for liquidity describes an inverse relation between interest rate and the demand for money. The quantity of money demanded declines as interest rate rises because the opportunity cost (interest foregone) of holding money is high. The M_D curve comes closer and closer to the vertical axis.

Conversely, at lower interest rates, larger money balances will be held because the cost of holding money (interest foregone) is low. Keynes suggested the possibility of *liquidity trap* which refers to a situation when the demand for liquidity for speculative purpose is very high because the rate of interest is very low. Everybody wants to hold as much cash as possible in expectation of future rise in the rate of interest. Expansion of money supply by the government cannot lower the rate of interest below a certain point. The extra money released by the government is held by the public, i.e. it gets trapped in public hands. The rate of interest R_1 in the Figure is the minimum below which it cannot fall.

Now let us see what happens when the liquidity preference of a community remains the same and money supply increases. Given the M_D, when money supply is M_1 the money market is in equilibrium at R_2. There will be disequilibrium at any other rate of interest and the market forces will push the rate of interest toward R_2 . If money supply increases from M_1 to M_2, it will cause interest rate to decline from R_2 to R_1.

A major criticism of the Keynesian theory of demand for liquidity is that it does not explain how people form their expectations about future normal rate of interest. In order to explain the rate of interest it assumes the existence of a normal rate about which the actual rate gravitates. Thus, the theory assumes what it intends to explain.

Differences in Interest Rates: The theory of interest rate determination is studied with the assumption of one uniform rate of interest. However, in the real world varying interest rates prevail at the same time in a country. Thus, individual borrowers pay a higher rate of interest than corporate bonds just like corporate bonds carry a higher interest rate than government bonds.

Interest rate differentials pertain mainly to gross interest (or market rate of interest) though there can be differences in pure rate of interest. Pure rate of interest is defined as the rate received on riskless loan. The important causes of differences in interest rates are the following:

Risk Element: Rate of interest varies directly with the risk attached to the loan. Thus, lower is the risk, the lower the interest rate and vice versa. Governments can obtain loans at lower rates than private firms. In fact, investment in government bonds is risk-free (gilt-edged investment) and therefore the interest earned is almost pure rate of interest. The higher rate of interest earned from non-government agencies is a premium for risk-taking.

Duration of the Loan: Rate of interest differs with the term (duration) of a loan because duration is related to uncertainty. Thus, the shorter is the term of a loan, the lower the interest rate and vice versa. Lenders expect a higher rate of interest on long-term loans because the risk element is greater. Return on risk is a part of gross interest in addition to pure interest. Moreover, a short-term loan is more liquid type of investment and therefore the lender would be willing to charge a lower rate of interest.

Cost of Servicing Loans: Giving a loan often entails a certain cost of keeping records, making collections and sometimes resorting to legal measures to recover the money. These costs differ from borrower to borrower. It is administratively economical for a bank to lend large sum of money to an industrial company than to lend small sums to a large number of individuals. In general, the bigger is the loan with fewer instalments, the lower the cost per rupee of servicing the loan.

Monopolistic Advantage: Interest rate may differ due to monopolistic/oligopolistic advantages enjoyed by the lenders. A lending institution in a small town may have no competitors and the loan-seekers there will have to pay higher rate of interest than prevalent in a big city. Moneylenders in Indian villages provide a good example of such monopolistic advantage.

Inter-governmental Transfers

Transfers (tax sharing and grants) are used to correct vertical imbalances, i.e. mismatch of revenue and expenditure responsibilities of different levels of a government. However, before such transfers are effected, it should be ensured that taxes, duties and levies assigned to a government are being optimally tapped. Thus, tax effort, if not a pre-condition, should at least form part of the formula for transfers.

The need for transfers arises because the own revenues of a lower level government (through tax assignments and non-tax sources) are insufficient to meet the expenditure required for providing services allotted to it. The theory of fiscal federalism justifies inter-governmental transfers on the following grounds.

Fiscal Gap Correction: Fiscal gap occurs when there is a mismatch between the expenditure needs and revenue means of a government. Fiscal capacity and fiscal needs differ because geographical and climatic conditions are more favourable in some areas as compared to others. Hence, the access to revenue base varies from region to region. Similarly, per unit cost of services varies depending upon the nature of terrain and density of population. Sometimes, fiscal gap may occur due to inappropriate assignment of revenue sources and functional responsibilities.

Minimum Standard of Services: Transfers from a higher to lower level government may be needed to upgrade the existing level of services to ensure a common minimum standard across jurisdictions. For example, a state government may provide grants to municipalities to ensure a national standard in the provision of certain public services.

Inter-Jurisdictional Spill-overs: Spill-overs (or spatial externalities) occur where the benefits of a locally provided service spread to persons who are not legally required to contribute towards costs of the service. Municipal services used by floating population without paying municipal taxes is a case in point. Services the benefits of which generally spill over to neighbouring jurisdictions include public transport, subsidised educational and medical facilities, anti-pollution measures and parks and recreational facilities. Inter-governmental grants are a major and often the most practical way of correcting spill over effects.

Designing a sound system of transfers is of vital importance in the context of financial discipline. Central government may keep in mind the following broad principles so that amount transferred is equitably distributed among the states.

1. The scheme of transfers should be based on well-defined objective criteria so that financially weak states are adequately assisted. These may include size of population, level of economic development, availability of infrastructure and minimum service standards.
2. The system of transfers should be so designed that states are not discouraged to mobilise resources on their own. Contrarily, the system should contain in-built mechanism to promote internal mobilisation of resources and their judicious management. For this purpose, the following additional criteria may be adopted and given due weightage: tax effort, adoption of sound financial management, innovations in the provision of public services, and economy in expenditure.
3. The amount and frequency of transfers should be reasonably predictable. They should be pre-determined

rather than being open-ended. Transparency, through explicit and identifiable budget entries, should also be ensured.

Interindustry Analysis **See Input-Output Analysis**

Intermediate Consumption **See Final and Intermediate Products**

Internal Diseconomies **See Returns to Scale**

Internal Economies **See Returns to Scale**

International Bank for Reconstruction and Development (IBRD)

IBRD (popularly known as World Bank) started functioning in 1946 as one of the two international institutions agreed to at the Bretton Woods Conference of July 1944. The other Bretton Woods institution is the International Monetary Fund. During the negotiations which preceded the Bretton Woods Conference, the British, led by John Maynard Keynes (1883-1946), favoured a single organisation, an International Clearing Union to manage the world money so as to reduce international economic fluctuations as well as the fluctuations in the balance of payments of member countries. Negotiators from the USA preferred two organisations, a bank for long-term lending and a fund for short term lending. The proposals of the USA were ultimately accepted.

To begin with, the Bank was asked to assist the external financing of the reconstruction of Europe at the conclusion of World War II. However, it was soon realised that the resources of the Bank were too few and its organisation too new for this task. In the initial years of Bank's functioning, lending operations remained scanty for purposes of development. This low level of lending was due to its small lending capacity, its conservative management and the unsettled state of knowledge concerning the development process. Bank's financing was largely confined to large infrastructure projects, such as transportation networks, and it was criticised for being too cautious with the development needs of its poor members.

In 1956, the International Finance Corporation (IFC) was established to supplement the Bank by participating in equity financing in member countries. Again in 1960, a third organisation, the International Development Association (IDA) was created to offer loans to low-income member countries on soft terms and conditions. This soft or concessionary assistance is made possible by contributions to the IDA by the governments of high-income countries. The management of the Bank is thus enabled to offer rates of interest and loan maturities which take into account the nature of the projects financed and the ability of borrowing governments to service the debt. The IDA is financed by periodic government contributions. The Bank obtains the funds it lends from the paid-in portion of the subscriptions of member governments and from earnings on past loans. Member governments of the Bank are represented by governors who meet periodically to receive the annual report of the officers of the Bank and to conduct necessary business. Governors and executive directors vote in accordance with the voting power of the governments they represent. Voting power is related to the subscriptions of the member governments and is based on a formula which takes into account such factors as gross national product and volume of foreign trade.

Presently, the Bank is the world's leading inter-governmental organisation engaged in the external financing of economic development in less developed countries. Loans given by the Bank help to finance the imports needed to complete approved development projects. Its advice helps to determine the priorities, the scale and the nature of the projects financed by it and through the development assistance programmes of industrial countries, by private banks, regional development banks and sources internal to the developing countries themselves. While the Bank is a wholly independent international organisation operating under its own Articles of Agreement, the staff of the bank co-ordinates its work with the relevant agencies of the United Nations and other international bodies.

International Double Taxation **See Double Taxation**

International Finance Corporation (IFC)

A subsidiary of World Bank created in 1956 to invest funds in private enterprises without government guarantees.

International Liquidity **See Liquidity, International**

International Monetary Fund (IMF)

IMF was established to promote international monetary co-operation through a permanent institution which provides the machinery for consultation and collaboration on international monetary problems. Specifically, the function of the IMF is to promote orderly and stable foreign currency exchange markets, to facilitate international trade and to contribute to balance of payments adjustment. To further these objectives, the IMF makes financial resources available to its member countries in times of balance of payments difficulties.

The IMF's charter embodied in the Articles of Agreement was agreed upon at the International Monetary and Financial Conference held at Bretton Woods, New Hampshire, in July 1944. In December 1945 the required number of countries had ratified the agreements, and in March 1946 the first meeting of the Board of Governors was held. The IMF commenced operations on March 1, 1947 at its headquarters in Washington DC

Important events in the history of IMF include: May 1948, first drawing by a member country; January 1962, adoption of the general agreements to borrow (GAB), which constituted an important supplement to the IMF's financial resources; February 1963, establishment of the compensatory financing facility, designed to assist countries that experience a temporary shortfall in export earnings; June 1969, inception of the buffer stock facility that can be used to finance commodity stockpiles; July 1969, adoption of the first amendment to the Articles of Agreement, providing for the allocation of special drawing rights (SDR) to member countries, with the first allocation of SDRs made on January 1, 1970; September 1974, implementation of the extended fund facility, designed to assist countries with medium-term assistance to overcome structural balance of payments problems; April 1975, establishment of an oil facility to help oil-importing countries to finance the increase in petroleum prices; February 1976, establishment of the trust fund, funded by revenues from gold sales, to aid developing countries with low interest assistance; April

1978, adoption of the second amendment to the articles providing for liberalised exchange arrangements, the legalisation of floating exchange rates, steps designed to eliminate the role of gold in the international monetary system, and enunciation of the goal to make the SDR the central international monetary reserve asset.

Rules and procedures of IMF are determined by the Executive Board and carried out by the staff. The voting power of each member country is determined by its quota, which is based on a complex formula that takes account of the country's size and its general importance in world trade and finance. In addition, each member country's quota determines the amount of financial resources it has to make available to the IMF (subscription) and its access (drawing rights) to the Fund's facilities.

Each member country is required to make available to the IMF an amount of funds equal to its quota. In turn, IMF member countries may utilise the Fund's resources if they find themselves in balance of payments difficulties. Technically, a member country will use its own currency to purchase other currencies (or SDRs) held by the IMF. Drawings made under the so-called credit tranches are subject to conditionality, i.e. the imposition of certain performance criteria by the Fund. Repayments to the IMF are normally to be made within 3 to 5 years, but under the extended facility the country may have up to 8 years to repurchase the foreign currencies advanced.

Much of the IMF's work is centred around annual consultations with each member country to ensure that its national policies are directed toward the goals of fostering economic growth, price stability, orderly financial conditions and the avoidance of unfair exchange manipulations. To ensure compliance with these basic tenets, the Fund is empowered to exercise firm surveillance over the exchange rate policies of member countries. The precise meaning of the surveillance function is still evolving and will, to a large extent, be instrumental in determining the future role of the IMF in the international monetary system.

The IMF's membership now numbers 182 countries. Membership is open to every country that conducts its own foreign policy and is willing to adhere to the IMF charter of rights and obligations. All major countries are now members of the IMF. The formerly centrally planned economies of Eastern Europe and the former Soviet Union have become members and are well on their way to becoming market economies. Members can leave the IMF whenever they wish. Cuba, Czechoslovakia (now the Czech Republic and Slovak Republic), Indonesia, and Poland have in fact done so in the past, although all these countries, with the exception of Cuba, subsequently reconsidered their decisions and eventually rejoined the institution.

On joining the IMF, each member country contributes a certain sum of money called a quota subscription as a sort of membership fee. Quotas serve various purposes. First, they form a pool of money that the IMF can draw from to lend to members in financial difficulty. Second, they are the basis for determining how much the contributing member can borrow from the IMF or receives from the IMF in periodic allocations of special assets known as SDRs (special drawing rights). The more a member contributes, the more it can borrow in time of need. Third, they determine the voting power of the member. The IMF itself, through an analysis of each country's wealth and economic performance, sets the amount of the quota the member will contribute. The richer the country, the higher its quota. Quotas are reviewed every five years and can be raised or lowered according to the needs of the IMF and the economic prosperity of the member. In 1945, the then 35 members of the IMF paid in $ 7.6 billion; by 1997, IMF members had paid in more than $ 200 billion. USA, world's largest economy, contributes most to the IMF, providing about 18 per cent of total quotas (around $ 38 billion); the Marshall Islands, an island republic in the Pacific, has the smallest quota, contributing about $ 3.6 million.

The founding nations reasoned in 1944 that the IMF would function most efficiently and decisions would be made most responsibly by relating members' voting power directly to the amount of money they contribute to the institution through their quotas. Those who contribute most to the IMF are therefore given the strongest voice in determining its policies. Thus, USA now has about 265,000 votes, or about 18 per cent of the total; the Marshall Islands has 275.

Although the IMF was founded primarily as a co-operative institution to oversee the international monetary system, it also supports that system by occasionally injecting into it sums of money, sometimes on a very large scale, through loans to its members. Indeed, the IMF is perhaps best known to the general public for pumping billions of dollars into the system during the debt crisis of the 1980s and for the vast amounts it committed to Mexico and to Russia during the 1990s. During 1983 and 1984, for example, the IMF lent some $ 28 billion to member countries having difficulty meeting their financial obligations to other members. In 1995, it extended to Mexico a credit of over $ 17 billion and to Russia more than

$ 6.2 billion to help tide these countries over a difficult period of reform.

The swift and well-publicised reaction of the IMF to this crisis might have misled observers into imagining that the IMF is first and foremost a lending institution. This is not the case, as the IMF remains primarily a supervisory institution for co-ordinating efforts to achieve greater co-operation in the formulation of economic policies. Nevertheless, its financial function is a significant activity.

Commodity Tranche: IMF makes credit available more automatically to countries which suffer a fall in their export proceeds due to decline in export prices. Commodity tranche refers to one-fifth of a country's quota in the IMF to which different rules and more automatic access applies than to credit tranche. ***Credit Tranche:*** Any borrowing by a country from IMF which is more than its automatic right of 25 per cent of its quota is called credit tranche (a slice of loan). These loans are allowed only if the borrowing country is taking appropriate measures to adjust its balance of payments deficit such as anti-inflationary monetary/fiscal policies. When the holding of a country's currency by IMF reaches 200 per cent of its quota, the country is said to have reached the limits of its credit tranche. ***Gold Tranche:*** Any country may automatically borrow up to 25 per cent of its quota in the IMF. This automatic drawing right is called the gold tranche. It is so called because this 25 per cent is equal to the quota which had to be deposited as gold by each member country in the IMF.

International Tax Avoidance and Evasion

The problem of international Double Taxation (q.v.) has an opposite face, viz. international tax avoidance (through legal means) and evasion (through illegal means). Two devices generally applied for the purpose are: multinational Transfer Pricing (q.v.) and the use of Tax Havens (q.v.).

International Trade **See Foreign Trade**

Investment Allowance

It is a tax relief based on the value of expenditure on qualifying investment in new industrial buildings, plants, machinery etc. It provides tax benefit which is over and above the depreciation allowed for an asset. Investment allowance is designed to encourage entrepreneurs to expand production by investment. It is a kind of general subsidy on investment expenditure.

Invisible Hand **See Market Mechanism**

Invisible Trade

This refers to services like banking, insurance, transport etc. and unrequited transfer items in the current account of a country's balance of payments.

Iron Law of Wages **See Wages**

IS-LM Analysis

IS schedule is a locus of points representing different combinations of interest rates and income levels consistent with equilibrium in the commodity market. LM schedule is a locus of points representing different combinations of interest rates and income levels consistent with equilibrium in the money market. IS-LM analysis seeks to find the level of income and the rate of interest at which both the commodity market and the money market are in equilibrium.

Isocost Line

An isocost line represents various combinations of two inputs (labour and capital) which a firm can purchase, given its total outlay and the prices of inputs. The general formula is $LP_L + KP_K = E$ where L and K are labour and capital, P_L and P_K their respective prices, and E the given amount of money.

In the figure below, if the firm spends the whole of total outlay on capital, it can purchase 10 units of capital. Conversely, if total outlay is used for labour only, it can purchase 10 units of labour. Joining these two points by a straight line, an equal-cost curve of the firm is obtained. See also Isoquant Curve.

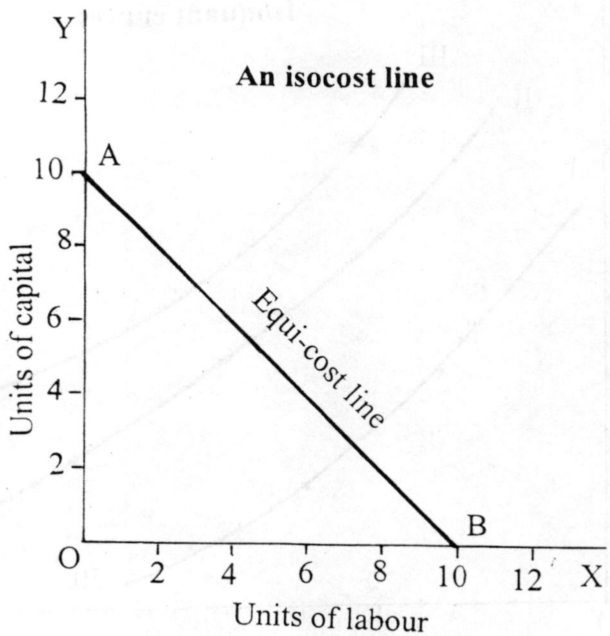

Isoquant Curve

An isoquant curve (also called equal product curve) shows various combinations of labour and capital with which a producer can produce a specific quantity of output. Analogous to indifference curves, a higher isoquant depicts a higher level of output and a lower one, a smaller quantity of output. Figure below shows various combinations of labour and capital which produce 100 units of a commodity.

The characteristics of an isoquant curve are the same as that of an indifference curve: (a) an isoquant curve slopes downward from left to right, (b) it is convex to the origin and (c) isoquant curves never intersect each other.

However, there is an important difference. Unlike indifference curves, we can specify cardinal measures of output to isoquant curves. For example, in the Figure below, isoquant curve represents 100 units of output. See also Isocost line.

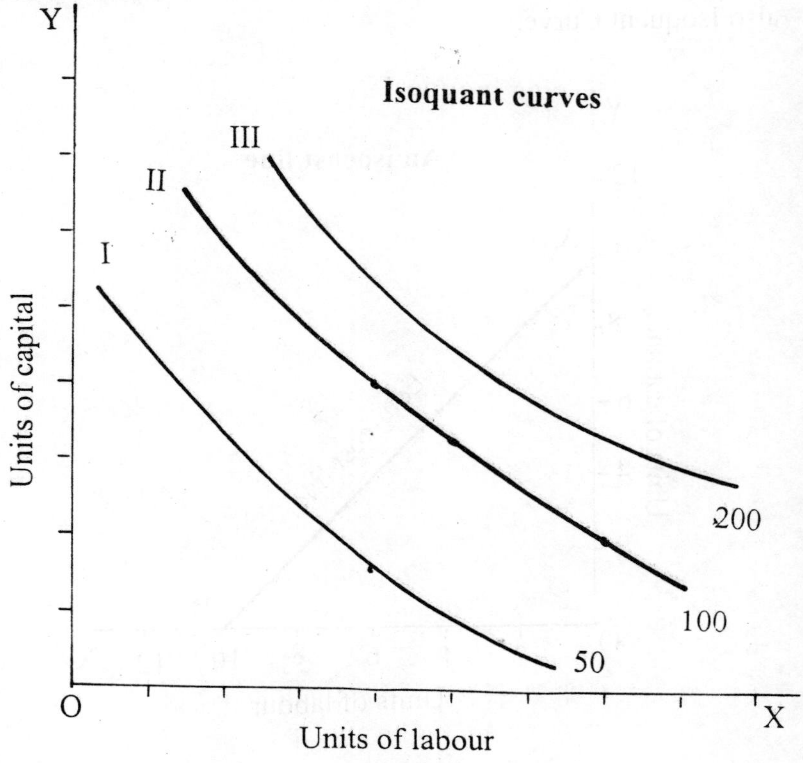

Itemised Deductions

In USA, these are payments that may be subtracted from adjusted gross income in calculating taxable income. These include, *inter alia*, medical payments, interest payments, state and local tax payments and contributions to non-profit institutions.

J

Jezzia See *Zazia*

Job Exports

It is a term used in connection with a country's multinational firms making investments abroad as a result of which job creation at home gets shrunk and jobs/employment opportunities are generated overseas.

Joint Assessment

It refers to aggregation of the incomes of husband and wife for joint assessment by tax authorities. See also Tax Treatment of Family Income.

Joint Occupancy of Tax Fields

It relates to concurrent taxation powers enjoyed by different tiers of government in a federal polity. Concurrent taxation powers are a characteristic feature of fiscal federalism in USA, Canada, and Australia. Most tax fields in these countries are jointly occupied by the federal and provincial governments. Thus, personal income tax, corporation tax, general sales tax, and consumption tax (excise duty) are levied by the Federal as well as Provincial Governments in Canada. The only notable exception is the customs duties which belong exclusively to the Federal Government.

The overlapping taxation powers often cause friction not only between the federal and provincial governments but also among the provinces *inter se* as regards the sharing of a

Tax Base (q.v.). The problem is solved through tax rental and tax sharing negotiations and agreements.

In India, the Central and the State Governments have no concurrent powers of taxation. Taxes with inter-state base and those in the case of which all-India uniformity in rates is needed to facilitate industry and trade are vested in the Central Government. Taxes which are location-specific and relate to subjects of local consumption are with the States. The absence of joint occupancy of tax fields has successfully minimised double taxation, duplicate tax administration, and tax rivalry between the Centre and the States, and among the States themselves.

Joint Venture

A joint venture is a business or industrial organisation set up by two or more firms by combining their resources, management and skill. It may be formed with a limited objective of undertaking a project or research work. Alternatively, it can be a multinational involving co-operation among different domestic and foreign companies. Joint ventures are different from mergers in that they involve the creation of a new business firm rather than a joint effort of two or more existing companies.

A joint venture may be set up by individuals, corporations, governments, or some combination of these three. Following are the examples of a joint venture: two large international oil companies jointly form a subsidiary to explore for oil in a region; a multinational firm establishes a subsidiary with local partners in a developing country to manufacture and sell in that market; a large manufacturing firm based in USA forms a joint venture with a state-owned enterprise in India; two firms agree to develop a new technology by creating a joint research and development subsidiary.

K

Kaldor-Hicks Compensation Criterion **See Welfare Economics**

Kennedy Round

General Agreement on Tariffs and Trade (GATT) aimed, *inter alia,* on reduction and stabilisation of tariffs on a reciprocal basis. To achieve this objective, member countries of GATT occasionally met and conducted negotiations for tariff reductions. Five rounds of multilateral negotiations were held between 1947 and 1962. During the period 1962-67, the sixth Round of negotiations was held which came to be known as Kennedy Round after US President J. F. Kennedy.

These negotiations were held in Geneva. After long debates between West European countries and the USA, an average reduction in tariff rates of around 35 per cent was agreed upon. This reduction was to be effected by all member countries in five stages during the period 1967-72.

Key Currency

It is also termed as reserve currency because of its use as an international reserve asset and also as means of financing international transactions. It is easily convertible into gold. Two notable key currencies are US dollar and British pound. Other important key currencies are French franc, German mark and Japanese yen.

Key Currency Country

It refers to the country whose currency is used worldwide as a reserve asset as well as for undertaking trade transactions. USA is one such country whose national currency, namely dollar is functioning as an international key currency.

The advantage to USA is that it is exempt from pressures of balance of payments deficit. It need not reduce its gold stock or its stock of foreign currency reserves as long as its foreign trading partners remain willing to accumulate balances in key currency (dollar) rather than to sell it in foreign exchange market. Thus, there will be no pressure on dollar to fall below its given exchange rate in response to the deficit.

Keynesian Economics

It refers to the economic ideas of British economist John Maynard Keynes (1883-1946) as propounded in his epoch-making book *The General Theory of Employment, Interest and Money* (1936) and other writings. Keynesian economics grew out of the turmoil caused by the Great Depression (q.v.) of early 1930s. Keynes believed that government intervention in a free enterprise economy was necessary to ensure sustained economic development. He maintained that insufficient aggregate demand causes unemployment and excessive demand results in inflation. Therefore, government should manipulate the level of aggregate demand by varying the level of its own expenditure and taxation. For example, to avoid a recession, the government should increase spending on public works, reduce taxes, and provide easy credit. These measures would lead to more investment, higher employment and increased private spending.

Keynes rejected outright the classical reasoning that working of price mechanism would always bring economic activities to a level of full employment. He believed that in the modern day economic life aggregate demand can be insufficient to absorb all the products that industry would produce if the factors of production were fully employed. If the continuity of the circular flow of money is broken, a tendency toward under-employment of labour and capital emerges with a correspondingly low level of national income.

Keynes developed a new theory which was concerned with certain economic aggregates. He stressed the relationship between total income, total consumption, total saving and investment, and total employment. As a result of his work, new tools of analysis were introduced into economics which are valid till date to a large extent.

Kinked Demand Curve **See Oligopoly**